Henry Martyn Field

The Barbary Coast

Henry Martyn Field
The Barbary Coast
ISBN/EAN: 9783337039189

Printed in Europe, USA, Canada, Australia, Japan

Cover: Foto ©ninafisch / pixelio.de

More available books at **www.hansebooks.com**

THE BARBARY COAST

BY

HENRY M. FIELD

WITH ILLUSTRATIONS

NEW YORK
CHARLES SCRIBNER'S SONS
1893

Copyright, 1893, by
CHARLES SCRIBNER'S SONS

Press of J. J. Little & Co.
Astor Place, New York

PREFACE

MANY years ago I met in the heart of India a German missionary, who had not seen his native country in forty years. At last the way was opened, and he hasted across the sea to look upon the Fatherland once more before his eyes should close in death. But the visit was a disappointment, and he returned, saying with true German simplicity, "Europe is too narrow for me!" We smile at this, but might we not ask in all soberness, "Why Europe only?" Why indeed, when at Gibraltar we are in sight of an older continent, and even from Marseilles it is but a day's sail to Algiers, where we are in another world, under other skies, and among other races of men—a quarter of the globe that is old and yet new, as it is still a field of discovery; so that it has at once the charm of the known and the unknown, of history and of mystery? I have been four times in Africa: twice in Egypt (once up the Nile), and twice on the Barbary Coast; and each visit increases the fascination. In the perfect winter climate one lives in the open air, and I sit under the palms and see the world pass by. The picturesque life of the people is a study for an artist. I look on with amused curiosity, but soon there comes another feeling, a doubt whether in all this gay scene there is more of gladness or of sadness. Poor old Africa! I love her for her very woes: and if I sometimes drop into an undertone, and, in drawing with a free hand these African pictures, give the dark background, with the lighter figures on the canvas, it is to turn, if I may, the eyes of our more favored countrymen to a distant shore, that they may look with tenderness and with pity on a land of so much beauty and so much sorrow.

CHRISTMAS, 1893.

CONTENTS

CHAPTER I
'TIS BUT A STEP TO AFRICA 1

CHAPTER II
DEAR OLD GIBRALTAR—THE BLACK WATCH 8

CHAPTER III
CARRYING THE WAR INTO AFRICA 25

CHAPTER IV
TAKING MINE EASE IN MOROCCO 32

CHAPTER V
PALACE AND PRISON 47

CHAPTER VI
FROM TANGIER TO ALGIERS 59

CHAPTER VII
ALGIERS 70

CONTENTS

CHAPTER VIII

The Robbers' Den 79

CHAPTER IX

In Grand Kabylia 88

CHAPTER X

The Gorge of Chabet 107

CHAPTER XI

Going Down into the Desert 120

CHAPTER XII

A Railroad across the Sahara 131

CHAPTER XIII

From Biskra to Constantine 144

CHAPTER XIV

Lights and Shadows of African Life 154

CHAPTER XV

How the Moslems Fast and Pray . . . 165

CHAPTER XVI

Lion Hunting in Numidia 175

CHAPTER XVII

The Last Great Man of Africa 182

CHAPTER XVIII

GOOD-BY TO ALGERIA 204

CHAPTER XIX

TUNIS—ARAB AND FRENCH 211

CHAPTER XX

THE FALL OF CARTHAGE 229

CHAPTER XXI

A SOUND OF WAR 250

ILLUSTRATIONS

THE GORGE OF CHABET	*Frontispiece*	
THE LIGHT-HOUSE AT CAPE SPARTEL	*Facing page*	42
A STREET IN THE OLD TOWN OF ALGIERS	" "	70
AN ARAB SCHOOL	" "	78
EL KANTARA : THE GATES OF THE DESERT	" "	120
AN AFRICAN PET	" "	124
CARAVAN LEAVING BISKRA	" "	131
IN THE DESERT OF SAHARA	" "	138
CONSTANTINE	" "	148
PRAYER IN THE DESERT	" "	172
A STREET IN TUNIS	" "	212
THE ANCIENT CISTERNS AT CARTHAGE	" "	234
THE SULTAN OF MOROCCO	" "	254
CAVALRY RETURNING WITH THE HEADS OF REBELS	" "	256
MAP OF THE BARBARY COAST	*At end of volume*	

THE BARBARY COAST

CHAPTER I

'TIS BUT A STEP TO AFRICA

GIBRALTAR is the stepping-stone to Africa, and Gibraltar is but a step from America. So it seems if one sails direct for the Mediterranean, instead of taking the long and roundabout way through England, France, and Spain. It is but little over a week from shore to shore. The voyage is not tedious, but restful. After a long strain of hard work, there is nothing so quieting to nerves and brain, as to lie on deck, stretched in a steamer chair, and look off with dreamy eyes upon the distant horizon. Every league that is left behind lightens the strain. The winds blow care away. Though it was winter—a winter of shipwrecks—the storms had swept the ocean farther to the north; and as we bore to the south, it grew warmer day by day, till the portholes were all open, and the air that floated in was that of June.

Nor was all the sunshine without: we had sunshine within. With a good ship, the Fulda, and a brave captain, we had also an agreeable company. The first man who faced me at table was a late member of Congress from Massachusetts, Mr. John E. Russell, who prefers the pleasure of travel to a seat in the Cabinet, and is going abroad with his wife to pass a few months in the south of Europe. Next to me sat Richard Harding Davis, one of the most popular of the young writers of our country. A party of twenty had their faces set toward Jerusalem, and a sad-eyed priest was returning to Rome. I observed him as the man who never smiled. Perhaps he could not after seeing the wickedness of America. He always sat apart on deck at the hour of sunset, apparently absorbed in his devotions, perhaps repeating his Ave Maria. Nor did I wonder at his being moved in such a presence and at such an hour, as he looked off upon that unceasing worshipper, the ever solemn sea, which, in its slow, measured, rhythmic movement seems like a mighty organ, through which the tempests breathe their anthems of praise; and over which, when it sinks to rest, the sunset flames as if it were nature's evening sacrifice.

In mid-ocean the monotony of the voyage was broken pleasantly by passing through the Azores. The first island to show its rugged front was Flores, nine miles long, rising boldly and abruptly from the sea, a formation which indicates that it was thrown up by a volcanic eruption, and is really the crest of a submarine mountain, which, if fully exposed, would be one of the highest on the globe, as the ocean around it is the deepest, having been sounded to a depth of four miles. The darkness came upon us as we swept along its shores, but the morning showed us another island still larger and more populous.

I had left word with the steward that I should be called at the first sight of Terceira. I slept with one eye open, and one ear too, to catch his footstep. It was still dark when there came a tap at my door, and in five minutes I was muffled up in a thick overcoat, and on the bridge with the captain. The sun was not up; the waning moon was still above the horizon; but there was an inexpressible beauty in the coming on of daylight over the sea. As it touched the cottages on the hillsides, it drew forth the simple people to see the great steamer floating by; the maidens waving their handkerchiefs to us as we passed, to which the captain responded with salutes from his steam whistle. It would have been a pretty scene at any hour, but it needed that soft morning light to make it so exquisite.

The island is twenty miles long, and its hillsides presented a succession of villages from one end to the other, whose whitewashed houses shone brightly in the morning sun. In the centre of every village stood the church, and here and there a convent, showing the devout faith of the Portuguese inhabitants.

The land is highly cultivated, and divided off into little plots of ground, like the fields of wheat and barley in Palestine. Already the spring-time had come, and the landscape was "dressed in living green." Flocks of sheep were feeding on the very tops of cliffs that came down in sheer precipices to the sea, while in the interior large herds of the broad-horned cattle find abundant pasturage. The volcanic soil here, as around Vesuvius, is favorable to the cultivation of the vine, which flourished greatly till the vineyards were literally eaten up by the *phyloxera*, which has proved as destructive here as in France. This destroyed the chief industry of the island. Then the people took to raising sugar, but the price has been so reduced in other countries that it yielded little profit. From sugar they turned to sweet potatoes, which they raised not so much for food, as to be distilled into a spirit that is shipped in large quantities to other countries, to furnish a basis of alcohol for wines and brandies, that are sold at high prices as absolutely pure! Whatever profit this may bring to the islanders, it can do no good to the countries abroad. But there is no such drawback on the oranges and lemons, which grow abundantly, and are as rich and luscious as those of Palermo, and furnish a large article of export to Europe and America.

But with all the resources that are left them, the people are very poor; and as, in spite of their poverty, they multiply like the children of Israel in bondage, some families having eighteen or twenty children, there remains no resource but emigration, which is chiefly to South America, where they find their own race and religion. The captain had been to Terceira no less than five times to take off companies of emigrants to Brazil. He described the parting scenes as most affecting when the poor people crowded on board to take leave of their kindred. Parents clung to their children, and sisters to their brothers, whom they might never see again. Amid them all stood the priest, with the people pressing round him, to kiss his hand or his robe, and receive his blessing. After such a picture, who could pass the miles of cottages in which these simple, loving, trusting people live, without a kindly thought of those who, in their humble homes, love each other with an intensity not always to be found in the dwellings of the rich and the proud? It is this mutual tenderness that sweetens human existence in cottage or castle, without which life is not worth living.

But the Azores are not wholly given up to poverty and destitution. On our left is an island which, though not in sight, and though it be the smallest of the group, is the richest of them all in its natural productions. Unlike its larger sisters, it is not of volcanic formation, and therefore not all hill and mountain, but one broad plain, a little above the level of the sea, and with a soil that bears everything. This gem of the Azores fitly bears the sweet name of Graciosa.

On the other side of our course, but not too far south to be seen, lies the flourishing island of St. Michael, the richest of all the group in commerce, as Graciosa is in agriculture. Its harbor is the chief seaport of ships sailing in these seas, as it is protected by an enormous breakwater, behind which they can take refuge from the storms that are sometimes very destructive in this part of the Atlantic.

The town has a large population, with many signs of wealth in the beautiful villas that peep out from the foliage on the surrounding hills. Some of these have extensive gardens planted with all kinds of trees. In the interior are fine roads that are carried along the sides of mountains, with many an outlook on the encircling sea. On these rugged heights there are forests of pines, while on the sunny slopes nearer the sea, and in sheltered nooks, the palm grows as in Egypt. Thus

> "The palm tree whispers to the pine,
> The pine tree to the palm."

Such pictures of this happy island made us regret to pass it in the night—a regret that we had also for Fayal and for Pico, which takes its name from the peak, over seven thousand feet high, that is visible sixty miles away.

However, the brief and hasty glimpses that we caught of these islands have made them familiar, so that the

Azores are no longer distant and unknown parts of the globe. One day's sight has brought them nigh to us, and henceforth they are our neighbors and friends, and we shall always have a tender feeling for the islanders who dwell in the midst of the seas.

As the last summit sank beneath the horizon, we bore away into the open sea. A day's sail to the south would have brought us to Madeira. But, as we were bound in another direction, the ship was swung more to the east, bearing straight for the Mediterranean. On Sunday afternoon we came in sight of Cape St. Vincent, the southwestern point of Portugal, a bold promontory which would be like the white chalk cliffs of England, except that here the cliffs are red, a fitter color for the scenes of blood that they have looked down upon: for it was off this cape that a great naval battle was fought in 1797, in which Nelson, though not the highest in command, greatly distinguished himself; and here, eight years after, he lay with his ships behind this rocky wall, waiting till the French and Spanish fleets came out of Cadiz, when on this same coast, a hundred miles below, was fought the greater battle of Trafalgar.

We were now approaching the Straits of Gibraltar, and the captain slacked his speed, not wishing to enter till daylight. I told Fritz to waken me as soon as we made the land. He came as before, and when eight bells struck, which to a seaman means four o'clock, I was on the bridge, with no companion but the captain and the cat, which appreciated our lonely situation, and came purring at our side. As we were to have a long wait, the captain took me in his room for a cup of coffee, when we resumed our watch. The stars were shining so brightly that the shores on either side were distinctly visible. The first light-house was that of Tarifa, the most southern point of Spain. Then appeared a light on the opposite coast, to be followed by that on Europa Point, at the very end of Gibraltar. One by one the passengers had crept upstairs, but it was not till we were between the two Pillars of Hercules, and just turning into the bay, that Richard Harding Davis, who has the frame of an athlete and had slept like a trooper, stalked on deck as if still not quite awake; and, turning his big head slowly round from one side to the other, asked, as if somewhat bewildered, "Where is Europe? And where is Africa?"

And so we glided gently to the haven where we would be. The voyage did not seem long; indeed, it would have been a pity had it been shorter. We left New York on a Saturday, and on a Monday morning, after one week at sea, dropped anchor in front of the Rock of Gibraltar just at the firing of the sunrise gun.

CHAPTER II

DEAR OLD GIBRALTAR—THE BLACK WATCH

GIBRALTAR was familiar ground, and as soon as I stepped on shore I was at home. There was the same varied life that had bewildered and bewitched me before. In walking up Waterport Street, one sees all colors and races—Jew and Gentile, Spaniard and Moor, Arab and Turk in their turban and fez, with the Maltese and Levantines seen nowhere but on the Mediterranean. It was a constant entertainment to hear them jabber, though I understood not a word, while the military elements had to me a great fascination. I liked to see the red coats, and to hear the rub-a-dub, and the blast of the bugle, and the tramp, tramp, of armed men.

Coming back to a place which interested me so much six years ago that I wrote a book about it, I find the official population almost wholly changed. The old regiments are gone. The former Governor is dead, and so, I am told, is General Walker, the veteran survivor of Indian and Crimean wars; and Lord Gifford, the Colonial Secretary, who was so polite to me, is in service elsewhere.

In the fortifications, also, I find a good many changes. The first object of interest to a stranger is the galleries in the Rock, cut during the famous siege a hundred years ago, to serve as casemates, from which the garrison could pour down shot and shell upon the Spanish besiegers, making their approaches on what is now the neutral ground. But on my present visit the galleries did not look so formidable as before, and to many of the embrasures there were no guns. I was puzzled, and feared that I had exaggerated the extent of these galleries or their importance. But the mystery was soon explained. The long galleries that I visited before are now closed to the public, which is amused with a meagre show of but half a mile. What is half a mile of guns when you looked for two miles?

The same exclusion is extended to a large part of the fortifications, to *all* the new constructions, and to the most vital parts of the old. The stranger is no longer permitted to ride his mule along the zigzag path up the mountain-side to the signal station, nor to stand on the plateau of the Rock gun, nor climb to O'Hara's Tower. The limits to which he may go are fixed, and the guards have strict orders to let no one pass who is not in uniform. In some places he may look, but not take any picture or photograph. Even in the old part of the town there are many things which a visitor may lay his eyes upon, but he must keep what he sees only in his memory. No artist may sketch an overhanging rock that he finds a picturesque point of view, but on which may be mounted a battery that the authorities desire to have concealed. No amateur must take snap shots with his kodak, unless he wishes to have a heavy hand laid upon his shoulder.

The reason for this rigid restriction it is easy to understand. The question for England is the defence of the greatest fortress in the world, and a defence against forces many times greater than Eliott withstood a hundred years ago.

Within the last twenty years, ever since the Franco-

Prussian war, military men in Europe have been exercised with the question of attack and defence both on land and sea. Wooden ships have been replaced by ironclads, in which the guns are fewer, but heavier, throwing shot to greater distances and with more destructive effect. The old fortresses were made of stone walls, which would not stand an hour against modern artillery. At last it came to the question, whether Gibraltar itself was safe. It had once made an immortal defence, but what chance would Eliott have stood if a line of ironclads had sailed up alongside the King's Bastion, against whose sides his hot shot would have been poured in vain? Even rock-ribbed hills are now torn to pieces by dynamite and nitroglycerine, and what might not happen if these new explosives and all the enginery of war, guided by some future Moltke, were turned against Gibraltar?

To determine the question of its defensibility, the English Government sent out a distinguished military engineer, who examined the Rock from end to end, and from base to summit, as the result of which he advised a double security, in the strengthening of the old walls by new and heavier guns, and the addition of another line of defences that is entirely new.

To carry out the first part of the plan, the number of guns has been diminished, but only to be replaced by a smaller number of greater power. In my walks about the town, I looked down from the Alameda upon a defender of Gibraltar that seemed not likely to be removed in any change of administration. To such a permanent resident, what in Boston would be called a "solid citizen," I could not be wanting in respect; and, republican as I am, I took off my hat and made a very low bow. It was the hundred-ton gun! Napoleon used to say that "power is never ridiculous," and this was the embodiment of power. Even Mark Twain could not make a joke of annihilation. Such a gun is a monster of destruction, a king of death. But though he is held in awe and receives an homage almost like worship, he is for the most part a dumb idol; he seldom clears his throat to speak, for the very substantial reason, that every time he opens his black lips he costs the English treasury fifty pounds—two hundred and fifty dollars! There are but few sovereigns in the world whose lightest word is worth so much as this. It is an event in the year when his thunder is heard. But the day that we arrived he was fired off three times. Was it a salute to a party of distinguished Americans? We will take it at that, and accept it in full of all accounts. Strange to say, as I was at that time in the galleries at the other end of the Rock, I did not hear it. But Davis, who was in that part of the town, says the explosion was like an earthquake. I am willing to take his word for it, and will not ask to have the experiment repeated.

With all the awe I feel for his iron majesty, if I were called upon to christen him, I should be puzzled to know what name to give him. "Destroyer" and "Peace Maker" are too common. Suppose we compromise on "The Last Argument," or General Grant's nickname of "Unconditional Surrender." British pride might like to call him "The Lion of Gibraltar." A lion he is, indeed, whose mighty roar shakes the very Rock itself. But do not wake him up, for if I were once to hear him, I am afraid I should consider it an immediate summons to the Day of Judgment.

This hundred-ton gun has a mate overlooking Rosia

Bay, and there are several of eighty tons that are placed along the line wall, on a level that will enable them, at point-blank range, to sweep the waters of the bay.

And now, in addition to all this, is being introduced an entirely new system of defence, not at the foot of the Rock, but on the top of it, making a mighty rampart of the very crest of the mountain. When this was begun, visitors and amateurs were shut out, that engineers might come in and have full sway. The work has been going on for years. Every point of vantage has been seized, and sharp rocks have been smoothed off for batteries, mounted with the most powerful guns known in modern warfare. To drag such guns to the top of the mountain was a work of incredible labor. Sometimes thirty mules were harnessed to a single gun; and if that were not enough, two hundred stalwart soldiers would add the strength of their lusty arms. This was indeed a pull all together; but with all this they could move but a few rods a day, so that it was weeks before a gun could reach its destined height. But at length they have got them in such number that they are planted at intervals all along the crest of the Rock, as if from this mountain height England would hurl defiance at a world in arms.

At the southern end, overlooking the Mediterranean, where once stood O'Hara's Tower, is now planted a gun, which, though not of such heavy metal as some below, is of prodigious range; indeed, I was told (incredible as it seems) that it would throw a ball fifteen miles! If so, it would fall in Africa. This would be a great achievement of military engineering; but, morally, would there not be something horrible in the very idea of the Pillars of Hercules thus stretching out their mighty arms across the Strait that divides them, the ancient Calpe hurling thunderbolts over the sea, to fall at the foot of Abyla, the Mount of God!

But while observing the picturesque figures in the streets of Gibraltar, I could not but recall, with renewed interest, the historical associations connected with regiments that have made themselves famous in all parts of the world. Of one of these in particular I learned a history that will be of interest to American readers. When I was here before, I had made the acquaintance of the Rev. Thomas Murray, the minister of the Scotch Church, and learned that he was still at his post. But I did not find him in the same home, for he had been "promoted" into a manse. I was glad that the goodly custom which obtains in dear old Scotland, that every minister have a roof over his head, is extending to the outposts of the Church abroad. It is not the same thing to live in a hired house, and move about from pillar to post, as it is to have a fixed habitation. Especially in a place like Gibraltar, where the military population is all the time coming and going, it is a little too much like living in a tent. But to have a house that is a part of the church property, and that cannot be alienated, gives the occupant a feeling of permanency, as if the whole establishment—church, manse, and minister—were anchored to the Rock itself. The manse is a Soldiers' Home, as they return from service in all parts of the world. The wandering Scot has not to inquire the way to the minister's, for the manse on Scud Hill is as well known as any private residence in Gibraltar, and he is free to knock at the door, sure of a hearty Scotch welcome, of a warm grasp of the hand, and of any kind service which it is in the power of the minister to render. Here I found Mr. Murray in his ample library, and in the midst of his charming family, engaged heart and soul in the work he has to do. A great sorrow had just come to him in the loss of a part of his congregation by the removal of a Scottish regiment, the famous Black Watch, which has been for the last three years stationed in Gibraltar. These brave Scots, though far from their native island, did not forget the " land of the mountain and the flood," nor the churches among the hills to which they had been wont to wend their way along the country side. A few of the officers belonged to the Church of England, but the great body of the rank and file were sturdy Presbyterians. These, of themselves, made a congregation that crowded pews and aisles to such a degree that the minister was obliged to leave his own church, and hold special services in a larger building erected near the barracks; and, here every Sunday morning, the gallant Highlanders, arrayed in tartan and kilt, marched in, five or six hundred strong, to worship God after the way of their fathers.

The regimental band supplied the music, not, of course, with the sound of fife and drum, or of trumpet and bugle, which would ill become the holy place, but with all stringed instruments.

And the singers, as well as the players on instruments, were there, not to sing any new-fangled verses, set to the light and trifling airs that make up so much of modern sacred music. Nothing would they have but the "Psaumes of Dawvid," which they sang in a volume which we might liken to the sound of many waters, only that no sound in nature is so thrilling as that of human voices, rising and swelling in praise and adoration. It was enough to inspire any preacher, and I envied my brother the privilege of speaking to such a host of armed men. Brave soldiers that they are, ready to face any danger in this life, they are not afraid to face the realities of the life to come; and so they relish good, strong doctrine, presented to them with a bold and manly utterance, such as their fathers were wont to hear when, in the days of persecution, they met in the glens of Scotland to worship God.

But this happy relation was coming to an end. The recent troubles in Egypt had called for an increase of the English troops, and the Black Watch was put under orders. It left but three weeks since for Alexandria, but finding that the flurry was over, and that political affairs had reverted to their former state of tranquillity, they were ordered still farther away, down the Red Sea, and out into the Indian Ocean, to garrison the island of Mauritius.

The departure of such a body of men at one stroke took away, I will not say the better part, but certainly the larger part, as well as the more picturesque and interesting part, of the congregation of the Scotch Church, and was indeed a great loss to the pastor, who has had them for three years as a part of his flock—a loss which, however, may be made good, if they have as their successors in the autumn another famous Highland regiment, the Cameronians.

Meanwhile let us not forget the parting heroes. It is a duty, not only to them, but to ourselves, to keep up the traditions of glory as the most powerful stimulus to the heroic deeds and heroic virtues by which nations are saved; and so, while the sails of the ships that carried them away are hardly below the horizon, we may recall their memorable history.

So much had I been interested in what Mr. Murray

told me, that I asked him if he could direct me to any book that gave a record of the long service which had made the name of the Black Watch so famous in the military history of England; whereupon he took from his library a massive volume entitled, "A History of the Scottish Highlands, Highland Clans, and Highland Regiments," * from which I have gleaned a few facts that I put on record in memory of those who once fought for us "in the brave days of old."

The Black Watch had its origin in a public necessity, growing out of the disturbed condition of Scotland at the beginning of the last century, when the distance from England was ten times as great as now, that in a few days, or even a few hours, an army can be transported to the border. Then the Highlands were very far away, and inhabited by a bold, independent, and somewhat lawless race, more ready to follow the chiefs of their clans to the field than to yield obedience to England. In 1715 they had been in open rebellion, and might be again. To guard against such an event, the men of substance, whose chief interest was that of general tranquillity, joined to form half a dozen independent companies, of not more than a hundred men each (three of them had only seventy-five), that were posted about the country in small detachments, to overawe any turbulent elements and preserve the peace of the realm. They were composed entirely of Highlanders, and were picked men, of a higher station than soldiers generally, the sons of good families, who had not only a country to fight for, but an honorable reputation to sustain. That they might not be wanting in military bearing, "special

---

* Published by A. Fullarton & Company in Edinburgh and London.

care was taken to select men of full height, well proportioned, and of handsome appearance." They retained the Highland dress, the most conspicuous feature of which was the broad tartan plaid that was wound about their bodies. This was sometimes called the belted plaid, because it was bound by a belt to the body so tightly that it was like the ancient girdle about the loins, by which every muscle was strung to its utmost tension. In this belt could be thrust the dirk and pistols, worn by him who could afford to buy them, for they were not a part of the soldier's kit. Thus accoutred in tartan and kilt and blue bonnets, they made a gallant sight when drawn up on parade or set in battle array. To distinguish them from the regular soldiers, who were sometimes called Red Coats, because their coats, waistcoats, and breeches were of scarlet cloth; the tartans of the Highlanders were of more sober colors—black, green, and blue —which gave them, when drawn up in long lines, a dark and sombre appearance, from which they were christened the Black Watch, a name which they were to make famous through the greater part of two centuries, on a hundred battle-fields, in every quarter of the globe— Europe, Asia, Africa, and America.

As the regiment was composed of independent companies, raised for a local purpose, that of self-protection, its first duty was at home, in Scotland; and it was with a reluctance that amounted almost to mutiny that it was marched into England, and finally took service in foreign countries, where it soon distinguished itself at the battle of Fontenoy, in which it was, for the first time, pitted against the French, whom it was afterward to meet on so many bloody fields. The French had often met the English, but now found new adversaries who waged war with a fierceness they had not seen before. A French writer could only describe their style of warfare by comparing it to the elements, thus: "The Highland furies rushed in upon us with more violence than ever did a sea driven by a tempest."

This swiftness of movement and fury of attack must be ascribed, in part, to their native strength and endurance. It was the pure Highland blood. At the battle of Fontenoy there was not a man in the regiment that was born south of the Grampian Hills. Coming of a rugged race, they were brought up to every kind of hardihood. Always climbing the mountains, they acquired the agility of chamois in leaping from rock to rock, and went up the mountain sides with a bound that carried them over other heights when they stormed the walls of a city.

From 1749 to 1756 the Black Watch was stationed in Ireland, and, strange to say, instead of being an army of occupation in a hostile country, lived in the most kindly relations with the people, proving that the Scotch and the Irish are not natural enemies, but natural friends.

Then came a long period of service on the other side of the Atlantic. For eleven years the regiment was kept in the West Indies, or on the mainland, where it fought beside our fathers in the old French War. The events of that war have been cast into the shade by those of the Revolution, but these ought not to make us forget that earlier history, in which there were deeds of heroism that have never been surpassed. An officer who was in the attack on Ticonderoga says:

"The oldest soldier never saw so furious and incessant a fire. Fontenoy was nothing to it. I saw both. We labored under insurmountable difficulties. The enemy's breastwork was about nine or ten feet high, upon the top of which they had plenty of wall-pieces fixed, and which was well lined in the inside with small arms. But the difficult access to their lines was what gave them a fatal advantage over us. They took care to cut down monstrous large oak trees, which covered all the ground from the foot of the breastwork about the distance of a cannon-shot every way in their front. This not only broke our ranks, and made it impossible for us to keep our order, but put it entirely out of our power to advance till we cut our way through. I have seen men behave with courage and resolution before now, but so much determined bravery can hardly be equalled in any part of the history of ancient Rome. Even those that were mortally wounded cried aloud to their companions not to mind or lose a thought upon them, but to follow their officers, and mind the honor of their country. Nay, their ardor was such that it was difficult to bring them off. They paid dearly for their intrepidity. The remains of the regiment had the honor to cover the retreat of the army, and brought off the wounded as we did at Fontenoy. When shall we have so fine a regiment again?"

This magnificent courage should not be forgotten because it was shown in the backwoods of America. The English make much—as they ought to make—of the storming of Lucknow, in which, by the way, the Black Watch bore a conspicuous part, but it was in no such danger of annihilation as at Ticonderoga. How daring was the assault is best seen by the losses reported, which tell that " more than one half of the men and twenty-five officers were either killed or desperately wounded." The exact figures are: " 8 officers, 10 sergeants, and 297 men killed; and 17 officers, 10 sergeants, and 306 soldiers wounded." It would be difficult to find anything more heroic in the history of war.

In July, 1767, the Black Watch embarked at Philadelphia for Ireland, but in nine years were back again in the War of the Revolution, and took part in the battle on Long Island, when Washington was driven across the river, and followed by the British army to White Plains.

Again the tartan appears under Cornwallis at the Brandywine, and in South Carolina. It may gratify our national pride to read in this "History of the Highland Regiments," that the first time (and the last) that these dashing Highlanders ever ran before an enemy was when, by the rashness of Tarleton, the famous cavalry leader, they were thrown into the very centre of the fire of Morgan's famous riflemen, from which there was no escape but in instant retreat.

With the war ended by the acknowledgment of our independence, the Black Watch returned to England. But their country was not to enjoy many years of peace. With the breaking out of the French Revolution began a succession of wars that lasted till the fall of Napoleon. In 1809 the regiment was in Portugal, and formed part of the army of Sir John Moore in his famous retreat to Corunna, and fought in the battle in which he fell. Three years later it was in Portugal again, under Wellington, whom it followed through the whole Peninsular War, to Salamanca, Vittoria, and San Sebastian, till Marshal Soult was driven across the Pyrenees, and the French, instead of conquering other countries, had to look to defending their own.

On the return of Napoleon from Elba, the Black Watch was in Brussels, and among the first British troops that hastened to the front through the Forest of Soignes, where

> "Ardennes waved above them her green leaves,
> Grieving, if aught inanimate e'er grieves,
> Over the unreturning brave."

History tells how they marched to the field to the sound of the pibroch, giving the first blow at Quatre Bras, where they struck the wing of the French army under Marshal Ney so hard as to prepare the way for the great event of two days later, the victory of Waterloo.

And now Europe had rest for forty years save one, when came the war in the Crimea, in which the Black Watch won new distinction under Sir Colin Campbell at the Alma, and in the long siege of Sebastopol.

Hardly had they returned from the Crimea when they were ordered to India, to aid in putting down the mutiny which threatened the Indian Empire; and, under the same gallant leader, went up country by forced marches, to the relief of Cawnpore, and took part in the storming of Lucknow.

In 1873 the Black Watch appears on the Gold Coast of Africa, in the Ashantee war, where, instead of fighting on open plains, they had to cut their way through the jungle and the forest. How they went through these new obstacles, no one has told in more glowing terms than Henry M. Stanley, who accompanied the expedition as correspondent of the New York Herald, and wrote home to America: "Nothing could surpass the gallantry of the Black Watch. They moved along the well ambushed road as if on parade, by twos, firing by companies, 'front rank to the right, rear rank to the left'; and thus, vomiting out two score of bullets to the right and two score to the left, the companies 'volleyed and thundered,' as they passed by the ambuscades, the bagpipes playing, and cheers rising from the throats of the lusty Scots until the forest rang again. Many were borne back frightfully wounded and disfigured; but the regiment never halted nor wavered, until the Ashantees, seeing it was useless to fight against men who would advance heedless of ambuscades, rose from their coverts, and fled, panic-stricken, towards Coomassie."

Nine years later, in the autumn of 1882, the Black Watch appeared in another part of Africa—in Egypt, where they fought in the battle of Tel-el Kebir, which destroyed at one blow the rebellion under Arabi Pasha, and reëstablished order under the Khedive. Two years afterward the regiment formed part of the expedition up the Nile for the relief of Khartoum and the rescue of Gordon. The expedition came too late, but not until the Highlanders had given further proofs of their valor at Kirbekan, and in other engagements in which they lost many brave men and officers, whose bones are now mingled with the sands of the desert.

What a long record of service and of glory in every part of the world! But the noblest thing in the history of the Black Watch is not its courage, splendid as that was, but that it was not brutalized by war, nor its victories stained by cruelty. These gallant Highlanders did not think that one need be less a man because he was a soldier. Nor did they find it necessary to brace up their courage by drunkenness or by oaths. Falstaff's regiment "swore horribly in Flanders," and gave the Flemings lessons in beastly intoxication; but when it came to the Black Watch to be encamped in the same country and among the same people, it is recorded of them that "seldom were any of them drunk, and they rarely swore." Instead of being tumultuous, as soldiers are apt to be, they were so quiet and so orderly that the people of the towns petitioned to have this regiment quartered amongst them for their own protection, feeling that they were more safe and their property more secure so long as these brave Scots kept guard over them. The Elector-Palatine wrote to his envoy in London to thank the king for their behavior, for whose sake, he added, "I shall always in the future pay respect to a Scotchman."

Nor did the profession of arms destroy the tenderness of nature in their rugged breasts. When the Black Watch were in Germany, it is related of them that they made themselves so much at home among the country folk, that often a stalwart Highlander might be seen at a cottage door, playing with the children and taking them on his knees, perhaps thinking the while of his own "bairns" in the humble cottage in one of the glens of Scotland.

Happy was I to read the story of such brave men, and happier still am I to tell the tale to my countrymen in America.

Nor is my admiration qualified in the slightest degree by the fact, that in the War of Independence the Black Watch were a part of the troops sent across the sea to maintain the authority of England in her colonies. A soldier has not to choose the service to which he shall be ordered:

"Not his to ask the reason why."

If the Scots fought against us in the Revolution, they fought for us in the old French War. Hundreds of the Black Watch fell at the siege of Ticonderoga, where their bones are mingled with those of our own heroic dead, and the beautiful lake that ripples along that shore syllables the names of our Scotch defenders along with those of the men of Massachusetts and Connecticut. Even were it not so, who can stand but with uncovered head beside a soldier's grave? In the grave all enmities are buried; we remember only the courage and the devotion. Regret as we may the stern necessities of war, we can but admit that war brings out in splendid relief some of the noblest qualities of our nature—courage, patience, fidelity, self-sacrifice—qualities without which the human race and human history were poor indeed. The traditions of brave deeds and brave men are the common inheritance of all lands and all ages. I envy not the man who can read unmoved the story of the Black Watch charging up the heights of the Alma, or marching with quick step while the bagpipes were playing "The Campbells are coming" to the relief of Lucknow.

CHAPTER III

CARRYING THE WAR INTO AFRICA

This second visit to Gibraltar renewed the fascination of the first. Though one be not admitted to her inner defences, there is enough in the picturesqueness of the old Rock, with the history of the wars, battles, sieges, through which it has passed, to make it one of the most interesting spots on the globe. It is worth a visit, if it were only to walk along the ramparts to the King's Bastion, where Eliott took his stand on the decisive day of the great siege; and to climb Windmill Hill, where one stops at every turn to look down on the fortifications at his feet, and off upon the sea, and across to Africa, which beckons him from the other side.

That other side is the natural sequel to Gibraltar, and so, when I had been round and round, and paid my reverence to the dear old place, I sailed away, though still looking back with tender regret. But in crossing the Straits one needs to consult the barometer, for the Mediterranean is a treacherous sea. When the mighty Atlantic comes rolling in, the place of meeting of the waters " boils like a pot," and is as rough as the English Channel.

As in crossing we turned not only south, but west, the afternoon sun was shining in our faces as we approached the African coast, so that we did not see Tangier till it burst upon us as a vision of beauty, its white walls rising from the sea, and culminating in the Kasbah, which is at once the palace and the citadel, as it is mounted with guns, and encloses within it the residence of the Bashaw, who, as the representative of the Sultan of Morocco, is the governor of the city.

As the steamer anchored off shore, the boats came off for passengers, among which I observed one that bore the United States flag, and as it came under our stern, heard a voice calling my name, and the Consul's men sprang on board, seized my belongings, and transferred them to the boat, and away we flew like the wind.

At the pier was another crowd that would have laid hands upon me had I been unattended; but when the American representative walked up the stone steps, all fell back and made a passage, with not even a word, only an admiring gaze. It is not often that I am invested with such importance, though it be only by courtesy; and I appreciated the silent homage of these Africans, who thought I was somebody, and it may be well that I shall not remain long enough for them to be undeceived.

Though it takes but three hours to come from Gibraltar to Tangier, in that brief passage one is transported into a new world. It is not only the difference in the two places, but the people themselves are different—in figure, in color, in language, and in everything that belongs to humanity—so that at first it seems as if they were hardly of the same human race.

In passing through the gates into the city, we have another surprise in finding no carriage to take us to a hotel. But if any prince or potentate were to enter under this archway, expecting to make a royal progress through the streets, he would be disappointed; for there is not even a baby-carriage in all Tangier, nor a wheeled vehicle of any kind. There are no broad highways for chariots, while some of the by-ways are too narrow for a dog-cart. Wherever you go, you must take your chance in the street with horses and donkeys and camels. A loaded camel that comes swinging along will soon clear a passage; at least, it is prudent to get out of the way. The more common beasts of burden are the little donkeys, with panniers on their backs; and a donkey always has the right of way. Americans will observe the beautiful democracy of this Moorish city, in which not only are all *men* free and equal, but all men *and beasts* are on a level of perfect equality. A donkey may not be a voter, but he has the freedom of the city by right of his heels. He is as free and independent as any of our newly imported citizens. He is no respecter of persons, and would kick a prince as soon as a beggar.

All this would be amusing if the streets were not so abominably filthy. Artists may think that dirt is always picturesque, as in the " Spanish Beggars " of Murillo. But this is not picturesque; it is simply dirt. The pavements are mere cobblestones stuck in the mud, with hardly an attempt to make a smooth surface. It is not an extreme presumption that the stones lie as they were placed by the hands of the Moors when they were driven out of Spain, and on these stones are dumped all sorts of rubbish, till it seems as if only a tidal wave breaking over these shores could wash the city clean.

And so we get a double impression of quaint old Tangier, as we view it from without or from within. It is a city of contrasts and contradictions, that answers to the fable of " Beauty and the Beast." On the outside it is one of the most beautiful of cities: within it is the vilest; and the transition from one to the other gives me such a shock that I am almost tempted to say that the shining walls which glitter in the sun are but a whited sepulchre, full of dead men's bones and all uncleanness.

And yet there is a beauty of nature which man cannot destroy. There is always a charm in a combination of mountains and the sea, as in the Bay of Naples, or along the Riviera, where one sits under the shadow of the Maritime Alps, and looks off upon the Mediterranean. The same combination gives to Tangier the beauty of Amalfi or Sorrento.

There is another attraction which makes it beloved of artists—a peculiar atmosphere, that takes all glare out of the African sun; in which a brightness that would otherwise be too intense is softened by a light mist rising from the sea, which draws a fleecy veil over the sky, through which the sunlight comes in all the colors of the rainbow, but fainter and fainter, as they are tempered and subdued to the most delicate tints that ever ravished an artist's soul. For this Henri Regnault preferred Tangier even to Egypt, since he found here skies as brilliant as in the gorgeous East, to which this atmosphere gave an inexpressible beauty; and he chose it as the favored spot where he would make his sketches and put in his colors, rather than on the banks of the Nile.

One thing more only is needed to complete the attractions of Tangier—its climate, which is said to have the double value of being alike good for all seasons. We are apt to think of Africa as a country of such burning heat that it can hardly be endured except in winter. But Tangier is in the extreme north of the continent, and has the sea on two sides—the Mediterranean on the north, and the Atlantic on the west—so that the air is always kept stirring by a breeze from one or the other;

while the sirocco, which might come from the desert, is warded off by the Atlas Mountains. Thus protected by heaven from the folly and negligence of man, Tangier, with all its filth, is a very healthy city, the rate of mortality being less than in many of the European capitals with the best sanitary arrangements. My own experience is too slight for me to give an opinion, but I find here two American ladies of a well-known family in New York, who have lived abroad for twenty years, trying all countries and all climates, and have finally settled upon Tangier, as having a temperature so uniform, with such freedom from the extremes of heat and cold, that they can live here all the year round without going off to watering-places to brace up their languid frames. They have bought a site on one of the beautiful hills in the environs, where they can have a garden in which will grow all the semi-tropical plants and flowers; and have built a house in which, with books and pictures, they can pass a life of lettered ease, never pining for the great world, but too happy to be " far from the madding crowd;" and where, with glimpses of friends who come and go, they can look out upon the mountains and the sea, and pass their days in quietness and peace.

Is not this the very place that I have desired for a few weeks' rest? Here I am settled, outside of the walls, in a hotel that bears the pleasant name of Villa de France. It stands on the top of a hill which commands a view of both the city and the bay; and as my room is on a corner, with windows opening on both sides, I can see in different directions. To the south I look down on Tangier, with its mosques and towers, while eastward I look across the Straits of Gibraltar to the Rock itself, taking in a long line of the coast of Spain, with the mountains of Andalusia. This beautiful spot is the first on which I pitch my tent in my African journey.

"But apart from the scenery and the climate, and the quaintness and picturesqueness of the place, is there much to interest a stranger?" Yes; a great deal. There is always an interest in studying new races of men in whom we are all the while finding touches of a nature like our own—touches that make the whole world kin. And there is more interest in the living present than in the dead past. "A living dog is better than a dead lion." A living Moor is better than a dead Egyptian. I like to wander about the streets of a strange city; to look into the faces of the people; to see what manner of men they are; to what tribe of the human family they belong; their figure, color, and complexion, whether they be white, or black, or red; to see how they carry themselves; how they stand and walk; how they sit down and rise up, especially when they sit, as they do here, on their heels.

The best place in Tangier to see all this is right under my window, in the famous Soko, or market-place, to which the people of all the country round come on the market days of the week, Wednesday and Sunday, for what we in America would call a cattle show, though it is certainly not an exhibition of prize cattle. To walk through the crowd you would think you had stumbled upon a camp of gypsies, as you see them wrapt in their miserable garments, all tattered and torn, trying to pull their rags over them to hide their nakedness; and when they lie stretched on the ground, or crouching under their little black tents, it is a scene of poverty and misery that is pitiful to behold.

And yet the Soko is a place of business where a great

deal of money changes hands in the course of the day. Moving about in this very miscellaneous crowd are men who have an air of bustle and business. They are the cattlemen from the country, who have their flocks and herds, and who have come, some of them, from a distance of two or three days' journey, riding on horses or camels, driving their sheep or cattle before them to market. Here, in the Soko, they find the purchasers, to whom they dispose of what they bring, and depart with money in their purses; while the cattle that have fed on a thousand hills supply the place of the roast beef of Old England, in feeding the garrison of Gibraltar.

CHAPTER IV

TAKING MINE EASE IN MOROCCO

ALL is not dark, even in Africa. Even the poor have their pleasures. A day or two since, walking across the Soko, I came upon a little company of Moorish musicians, sitting on the ground, making a horrible din, that was enough to stampede a camel, but which so wrought upon the sensibilities of a poor old creature (whose tattered garments were dropping from his back, and who seemed to have one foot in the grave and the other sliding in), that he sprang up and began to swing himself about like a whirling dervish. The music (!) had literally " created a soul under the ribs of death." The incident, trifling as it was, showed me that this poor people, miserable as they are, are ready to be merry and gay on the slightest provocation.

The foreign residents are not so lightly moved. It is hundreds of years since Froissart wrote that "the English take their pleasures seriously;" he might almost have said solemnly, for when they do go about it, they undertake it as if it were the one business of life. English officers find the round of garrison duty very tedious, and are glad of anything to relieve the wearisome monotony. In a fortress like Gibraltar the range of pleasures is very limited, and men whose veins are full of hot blood must break loose somehow. They cannot fight a battle every day; but they can at least mount their horses, and dash off into the country at full speed, as if they were leading a charge of cavalry. And if there comes a holiday, when there can be a mingling of fair women with brave men, the scene rises to its highest point of joyous hilarity.

An illustration of this it was my fortune to see. We arrived in Gibraltar in the last days of the carnival, when the fun waxed fast and furious in anticipation of the coming of Lent, which would shut down like a pall on all life and gayety. As it is the fashion in all Catholic countries to make the most of these last days, they quicken the pace as the moments fly. On the Mardi Gras, the Tuesday before Ash Wednesday, the streets were thronged, like the Corso in Rome, with a good-natured crowd, that took all sorts of liberties with those who rode about in carriages, pelting them with bits of colored paper, and giving way to every extravagance of folly. Nor were the people of fashion any better, for they, too, made the most of the opportunity, and danced till midnight; and then, as the clock tolled the hour, fell on their knees, in token that the season of pleasure was past, and the season of prayer and penance begun.

The officers of the garrison took their pleasure, as became true Englishmen, in an English way, in a fox hunt. In the morning they might be seen trooping toward the gates, in many cases accompanied by their wives and daughters—for these English women are famous riders—and, crossing the Neutral Ground, the hounds were let loose, whereupon they quickened their pace to a trot, and then to a run; and with rush and dash, and shouts and laughter, sped away, to the music of hounds and horn, over the hills of Spain.

Who would not join in this gathering of the fair and the brave? My friend, Richard Harding Davis, went out with the riders, and when he came back, as I met him in his riding boots and spurs, he looked like a cavalry officer. I, too, had received the honor of an invitation; for it was intimated to me, as to him, that if I cared to join this gallant company, I should be heartily welcome as an American guest. Alas, that I could not support the honor of my country! I had to answer that my galloping days were over. The fact is, that my camel-riding on the desert has spoiled me for anything less romantic; and I qualified my refusal by saying that I would join in the general rout if they would bring me a steady old camel, mounted on which, like a venerable and long-bearded sheik, I would bring up the rear.

Here ended the first lesson. But I did not escape temptation by crossing the Straits of Gibraltar. Indeed, I may say that I ran into it, for the very reason that Tangier has less communication with the outside world, and fewer resources for entertainment. There is no turnout of carriages to drive to Hyde Park or the Bois de Boulogne, nor even a drive like that to Europa Point and back again, which gives the gay world a chance to look in each other's faces; for there is not even a "one-hoss-shay" in all Tangier, or, for that matter, in all Morocco. Hence everybody lives and moves, particularly *moves* on horseback. At our hotel are some English officers returned from India; and the talk of every dinner is the morning and afternoon ride, or, more exciting still, of some grand sport in the African forest.

Such is the prospect that we have before us, when for a week all Tangier is to be turned upside down to engage in a boar hunt. The country round is full of wild boars, some of which are very large and very fierce, so that to hunt them, if not as dangerous as to hunt the tiger, is by no means child's play; for when an old boar is driven to bay and turns upon his pursuers, rushing at them with his long tusks, he who is in front must be ready for the attack, or he cannot be too quick in getting out of the way. It is this spice of danger which gives to a boar hunt a degree of excitement that stirs the blood of an Englishman as a bull fight stirs the blood of a Spaniard.

To gratify this natural passion, some thirty gentlemen of Tangier, representing all the foreign legations, are going into the country, provided with tents, to make a regular encampment, and remain five days. They will be attended by a hundred Moors as camp-followers, some to pitch the tents and attend to the commissariat, while the others serve as beaters, to scour the woods and rouse up the noble game, and drive them toward the place where the hunters are waiting, mounted for the chase.

Such was the picture that was set before me, and how could a stranger listen unmoved to an invitation to join in a favorite pastime of the Prince of Wales and other illustrious patrons of the chase? I confess that the royal character of this peculiar form of amusement was a little taken out of it by a mere change of name from boar hunt to "pig-sticking," which describes more exactly what it is, for in the combat the assailants are confined to the use of the spear. No guns are allowed in camp, for if, as soon as an old tusker showed his head through the trees, some rifleman were to draw a bead on him, and drop him, the sport would be over in an instant; whereas the excitement is all in the chase, when thirty horsemen set off on a run, up hill and down, till at last the monster is laid low.

Such was the temptation that was set before me, to which I replied that I would take it into respectful consideration. As my readers are entitled to a full detail of my thrilling adventures in Africa, it would be fitting that, when I ride to battle, I should be attended by some one with a kodak, who should take a snap-shot at the instant that my spirited steed is rearing in air, while the rider is throwing the spear that is to lay the brute in the dust at his feet. This would make a companion piece to the picture of St. Michael and the Dragon. As I have often been requested to sit for my photograph, this is the attitude in which I prefer to go down to posterity.

Well, well, well! Is there really nothing but a fox chase or a boar hunt to offer to a sober old traveller, who in all this hurly-burly asks for nothing but to be let alone? I do not object to others amusing themselves after their fancy, but they will excuse me if I prefer to sit in the African sunshine, and hold quiet converse with the mountains and the sea.

Happily there is a variety sufficient for all tastes, and I find many a retreat fit for a philosopher. Two miles from the city is a range of hills, which surround it like an outer wall, on the brow of which some of the foreign ministers and consuls have their country places, to which they retire after the cares of the day. Here lives Colonel Felix A. Mathews, who has been the American Consul for more than twenty years, and here he delights to show hospitality to his countrymen at his house on "Mount Washington." As there is no way to get about in Tangier but on horseback, he sent me a horse, with a soldier to guide me to the place. Being by nature grave in my outward carriage, as in my inward mind, I had asked for a steed that should not be too gay; in response to which I found before my door a venerable creature, that seemed not at all likely to betray me into a speed inconsistent with my ministerial dignity. But a rider on a white horse is always a picturesque object in a landscape, and when I mounted and rode forth with slow and solemn pace, I thought I answered somewhat to the picture in the opening line of the Faery Queen:

"A gentle Knight came pricking o'er the plain."

To complete my knightly appearance, I had a military attendant. To be sure, he did not answer to my idea of a man-at-arms, with gun on his shoulder, or sword at his side. To confess the truth, he had no weapon of war of any kind; and as for his uniform, it consisted only of the *jelab*, an overall of very coarse cloth, which is the one garment which answers for all purposes in Morocco. It covered his body, but his head and legs were bare. But the absence of under garments, which exposed his naked limbs, did not detract from the grace of his person; for as the *jelab* hung but half way down his form, it showed a lithe and sinewy figure, on which there was not an ounce of superfluous flesh, so that he not only trotted easily by my side, but sometimes was so full of animal spirits that he bounded away before me, and cut all manner of capers as he sprang up every slope of ground that rose before us on our winding way.

In half an hour we were at the Consul's, a plain house, but made beautiful by being embowered in trees of his own planting, with a great variety from different countries and climes. He likes to unite those of Africa and America. Having come from California, he has introduced here the Monterey cypress, which flourishes beside the African palm. So kindly does it take to this soil, that it has been introduced on other places in the neighborhood, and its dark foliage forms a pleasing feature along the roads.

But the special charm of the day was the good company gathered at the hospitable table—ladies from New York, with whom I could talk of old friends; a physician from Philadelphia; and an American artist, who has come here to take the picturesqueness of African life, with the glory of the African sky. Will my friends at home think it strange if I confess that I had rather spend an afternoon in such a scene and in such company than to spear all the wild boars in Morocco?

The pleasure was repeated a few days after, in another excursion, with a friend to whom I owe much of the pleasure of my visit to Tangier. No one here is better known than Mr. Ion Perdicaris, who has lived here twenty years, and whose house in the city, built after his own design (in which he has introduced many features of Moorish architecture), is one of the most beautiful that I have ever seen. In addition to this, he has another house on the same range of hills with our Consul, though farther round the bay. Again I had asked for a mount of proper sobriety, a horse whose step was slow and stately; but that variety of beast is limited in this Moslem empire, and, instead, he brought me a blooded Arabian, that was a gift from the Sultan, though he said it was the most quiet creature that he had in his stables. I mounted with some apprehension; but my experience has shown that neither men nor horses are always as fierce as they are painted, and, indeed, I could not have desired a more gentle creature. He did not try to play any tricks on his new rider, but bore me so gently that I really forgot that he had not been brought up in the most strict rules of obedience. Thus mounted, trotting gently along the road and up the hills, with the best of company, what more could heart desire? The day was perfect. The week before there had been a good deal of rain. But now all was cleared away, and only a few fleecy clouds were floating over the blue sky. "What is so fair as a day in June?" asks Lowell; to which I answer, that no day in June was ever fairer, brighter, yet softer and sweeter, than this last day of winter.

The only drawback to the full enjoyment of the ride was the poverty of the people whom we met along the road. The men were poorly clad, often in rags; but the hardest lot was that of the women and children, great numbers of whom were tramping through the mud with bare feet, with bundles of sticks and brush upon their backs which they were carrying into the town to sell, for which they would receive possibly ten cents, though, I was told, more often but five. This was their compensation for the work of a day. Many of these were girls of but twelve or fourteen. What wonder that at twenty they are already old, or that sometimes they are betrayed by wicked men into sin? Then the law of the Koran, which is the only law of the country, shows them no mercy. She who once goes wrong is instantly an outcast, to be driven from her home, to be beaten or killed. "I have known," said Mr. Perdicaris, "three instances in which girls have been killed by members of their own family, because of such disgrace. One day I heard a shot near my house, and inquiring into it, I found that, on suspicion of this, a young Moor had shot his own sister. There was some pretence of calling him to account for it, but as it was said that he was the only son of his mother, and that she was dependent on him for support, that was quite sufficient to satisfy the Moorish authorities."

Those writers who make elaborate defences of the religion of Islam, should tell us why it has no mercy on the erring. Nor does it make any provision for the insane. As we were riding by a little village of low-thatched cottages, Mr. Perdicaris said: "A man from this village was in my employ, and a good, faithful fellow he was. But suddenly he was taken insane. What could be done with him? He needed to be removed at once to some place where he could receive medical treatment, or at least the common offices of humanity. But such a place does not exist. There is not an asylum or a hospital in the whole empire of Morocco; and the poor maniac had to be left in his miserable hut, where he was chained like a wild beast."

While thus talking, we were climbing up higher and higher, and the view beneath us was spreading out wider and wider. I wanted to stop at every turn to take in the full glory of the scene. After mounting to the top, and riding along the summit for a mile, we descended toward the sea till, on a shelf of land sufficiently below the height to be sheltered from the east winds, and yet hundreds of feet above the waves, we came to Idonia, which signifies the place of the nightingales, fit name for one of the most delightful retreats in which a man ever sought shelter from the cares of the outer world.

As with his house in town, Mr. Perdicaris designed this for himself, and laid out the grounds, which gives the place a character quite unique. Here, sitting on his veranda, he has the whole extent of the Straits of Gibraltar under his eye. To the east he can see the Rock itself, and, when the wind is favorable, hear the morning and the evening gun. Nearer still is Tarifa, at the very mouth of the straits; while a little farther up the Spanish coast, but in full view, is Cape Trafalgar, off which the great battle was fought. "When I first came here," he said, "there was an old Moor who remembered distinctly seeing, as he described it, a hundred ships, and seeing the smoke of the battle and hearing the thunder of the guns all day long." With such views and such memories beguiling the hours, we lingered and lingered, taking our luncheon under the orange trees; and then, enchanted with all the beauty of the day, rode slowly over the hills, and back to the city.

So captivated was I with this excursion that I was not content to leave Tangier till I might have it repeated, and extended still farther to the most picturesque spot in all its environs, Cape Spartel, where the light-house looks down at once on the sea and the ocean—the Mediterranean and the Atlantic. Colonel Mathews, eager as ever to contribute to the pleasure of his countrymen, offered to be my guide and companion. It was a beautiful morning when we started from his house and rode through the lanes that wind hither and thither, in a gradual ascent, till we emerged on the upland, where the high, rolling country, with its wealth of heather in blossom, reminded me of the moors of Scotland. For several miles we followed the same route that we had taken in the ride to Idonia, from which we continued five or six miles farther. Now, as then, the sky was without a cloud, and the atmosphere so clear that we heard distinctly the guns of Gibraltar, though it was more than thirty miles away.

But the mountains! the mountains! The horizon was so full of them that there was no counting them any more than counting the waves of the sea. And what set them in still grander relief, their sides sloped down into deep valleys, where, though the winter was but just past, the African sun lay so warm that the wheat and barley were already springing up, and the landscape was in its freshest green.

As we rode on over the hills, the scene grew more rugged from the masses of rock scattered here and there. Some of these had apparently been splintered by lightning, but still held up their broken shafts to the tempest. The only thing wanting was trees; but I suppose that nothing can withstand the storms that break over the coast. At least, I saw not a single great trunk on the crest of the hills. And yet it is not a rocky desolation, for even the rocks are so far buried in masses of heather or low underbrush, that they do not stand up in utter nakedness. And what is more remarkable, though the surface is so stony, the soil is admirably adapted to the vine, and nothing but cultivation is needed to cover all these slopes with vineyards as rich and fruitful as those along the Rhone or the Rhine.

A few miles farther, and we begin to descend toward the sea. And now, as we get under the shelter of the hills, we find not only a thick underwood, but goodly trees, till at last we are under an arch of green, through which we prick up our horses, and come out on an open space, and dismount in front of a building that looks like a fortress or a tower, but which is a light-house, the only one in Morocco, that at Cape Spartel.

It seems strange that an empire as large as France had not, thirty years ago, a single light-house! It had a coast line of hundreds of miles on the Mediterranean and on the Atlantic, a coast that was very dangerous to

THE LIGHTHOUSE AT CAPE SPARTEL

navigators. On the west the waves of the Atlantic rolled in with tremendous force, dashing ships against the rocks, or wrecking them on the sands; so that sailors who had been on distant voyages, and were returning to Europe, often perished almost in sight of home. And yet this had continued for centuries, and not a single watch-tower had ever sent a ray of light over the angry waters to warn mariners of the dangers of the sea. The point of greatest peril was at this shoulder of Africa, which is thrust out between the Mediterranean and the Atlantic, as ships are daily and almost hourly leaving or entering the Straits of Gibraltar. Nowhere in the world was a light-house more needed. Yet who should build it? England and France and the United States protect their own shores. But who should protect Morocco? It had not the same interest to protect itself. Perhaps it would not be altogether uncharitable to suppose that, in the good old times when the Barbary pirates carried on their trade along this coast, they were quite willing that Allah should send storms and shipwrecks in order to throw the richly laden ships into the hands of the true believers. But now that Christendom has driven piracy from the seas, there is no motive to wish that shipwrecks should be more frequent. All the commercial countries united in an appeal to the Sultan, who answered that Morocco had neither navy nor commerce, and therefore had no need of the security which a light-house would give. But, for all that, if the said powers would design such a structure as would meet their wants, and supervise its erection, he would pay the cost, the powers for whose benefit it was erected engaging to see to its maintenance from year to year. This was not only a fair, but a very generous offer, and was at once accepted. A French engineer was put in charge of the work, who, having *carte blanche*, did not spare expense, but used all his resources to build a tower that should stand any storm that blows. So far as a mere visitor could judge, he accomplished his purpose, for in appearance it is as solid as the rocky foundation on which it stands. It is a massive structure, with stone walls of great thickness, rising in a square up to the circular lantern. Of course we climbed to the top to inspect the great illuminator. As we looked out over the waves, we saw that it must sweep a vast horizon. The lamp itself is an object-lesson. It is a study to see how such a light is generated. We have been taught that any light, great or small, travels a good ways:

"How far that little candle throws his beams! So shines a good deed in a naughty world."

But here is a light that must be like a beacon fire on a mountain top, for which there are provided, I will not say "rivers of oil," but certainly barrels and hogsheads of the most illuminating oils in the world; and the light thus produced is not only doubled and quadrupled, but multiplied an hundred-fold by enormous reflectors, so that it is clearly visible twenty-five miles at sea.

This famous light-house we found in charge, not of a Moor (I doubt if there is one in all Morocco that would know how to attend to all the mechanism), but of a German who has been here for a great number of years, and who, though very simple in his manners, is a man of intelligence and scientific knowledge. He was of opinion that, long before the Christian era, the Phœnicians had not only passed the Pillars of Hercules, but sailed down the whole coast of Africa to the Cape of Good Hope, and returned by the Red Sea.

Though he is seventy-one years of age, he is so alert in body as well as in mind, that he thinks nothing of taking his cane and "skipping" over the hills ten miles to Tangier, and back again.

One of the things which the old man took a pride in showing us was his Book of Visitors, in which are some illustrious names. Among the earliest visitors (it must have been soon after the light-house was built, for it was more than a quarter of a century ago) appears this record of the Duke of Edinburgh:

"15th of January, 1866, Alfred [who, though under the head of 'Occupation' he is entered 'Prince,' had at the time the practical business of an officer in the British navy, so that further is added], H. M. S. [Her Majesty's Ship] 'Raccoon,'" with the brief comment: "H. R. H. [His Royal Highness] and party much pleased with the manner in which the light-house is kept."

More than twenty years later appears a still more illustrious name, no less than that of the Sultan of Morocco. Under the year "1889" is the following record entered by the keeper of the light-house:

"Aujourd'hui le 5 Octobre (a 9 heures du matin) a été ici S. M. Scherifitienne Sidna Muley Hassan à voir son unique Phare (dans tout l'Empire). S. M. a inspectionné tout en general, étant très aimable avec tous les employés du service et avec leurs familles.
"J. GUMPERT,
"*Guardien chef.*"

When all this sight-seeing was over, and the official business also—for the Consul, as representing one of the powers that contribute to the maintenance of the light-house (there are eleven in all, each paying annually fifteen hundred francs, or three hundred dollars), has to make an inspection several times a year—he invited us to a service which is always agreeable after a long ride.

I had observed in our train a donkey whose panniers seemed to be filled with a preparation for some festivity. When we were seated round the table, the Consul reminded us that it was the 4th of March, on which a new administration was to be inaugurated at Washington, and he desired us all to join him in wishing long life and health and prosperity to President Cleveland. We afterward learned, through the English papers, that he was inaugurated in a snowstorm, and wished that we could have sent him, and the crowds in the capital on that day, a little of our African sunshine. Certainly every true American, in whatever part of the world he may be, would join with a full heart in wishing all possible good to one who is at the head of the Great Republic!

The allusion to country and home set my heart quivering, in spite of my new-born enthusiasm for Africa; and I went out upon the rocks, and, leaning against one that stood upright, turned my eyes to the west, and gave a long, lingering look toward America. There it was, far, far away below the horizon; yet, for all that, strong and steadfast, the land of promise and of hope. I can never resist such a situation, and, before I knew it, I was repeating to myself the old words:

> "The breaking waves dashed high
> On a stern and rock-bound coast;
> And the woods, against a stormy sky,
> Their giant branches tossed."

Out of such storm and darkness came the wonder of history. Four hundred years have passed since Columbus first saw the Western shores, and in that time the unknown land has grown to be the light and hope of the world.

CHAPTER V

PALACE AND PRISON

"I stood in Venice, on the Bridge of Sighs,
A Palace and a Prison on each hand."

So wrote Byron of the City in the Sea—lines that have come to me here, as I stood on the Kasbah, which looks out upon a greater sea than the Adriatic, and that, under its white walls which shine so brightly in this African sun, hides a mass of human suffering as great as ever festered and rotted in the dungeons of the Palace of the Doges. It is a sad lesson, but may be a profitable one, to set in contrast this magnificence and this misery.

Soon after our arrival our Consul wrote that he had made arrangements to present me, with Richard Harding Davis, to the Moorish Minister of Foreign Affairs, and to the Bashaw, who is the Governor of Tangier. The day fixed was Friday, which is the Moslem Sunday, on which no business is done till after the hours of devotion, when it is taken for granted that all true believers are in the mosque, saying their prayers, during which time the gates are shut lest the infidels might steal in and capture the city! But at three o'clock their prayers are ended, and these high dignitaries would be happy to receive us. Accordingly, at that hour, Davis and I met at the Consul's office, and all together walked up the hill to the Kasbah.

We were first to pay our respects to the Minister of

Foreign Affairs, who, as soon as we were announced, came out to meet us—an old man, with a white beard, and a most kindly face—and welcomed us with true Eastern hospitality. Conducting us into a reception-room, he made us at once at home, taking a chair in the midst of us, so that we formed a little circle. His manner was so gracious and his countenance so benevolent, that we could not help flattering ourselves that his courtesy was a little more than formal as he asked after our welfare. The conversation then took a wider range, the burden of which, of course, fell upon the Consul, who speaks Arabic like a native, while Davis and I put in a word now and then, to give, or to receive, information. As we were warm in praise of the beauties of Tangier, he in return expressed his good wishes for our country, though his ideas about it were somewhat vague. The Moors know but little of foreign countries, except Spain, whose shores they see across the Mediterranean. Apparently all that the Minister knew about America was that it was a very big country, and very far away. As some allusion was made to the European powers whose ships of war had been lately in these waters, as if they had designs upon the independence of Morocco, Davis (the wicked fellow!) intimated that Morocco would be a match for them all! Then, venturing a little farther, as he knew that the Moslems have a great veneration for sanctity, he whispered to the Consul, with a twinkle in his eye, "Tell him that Dr. Field is a holy man," which he would understand as being a sort of Christian "mollah;" at which the Minister turned reverently to me, and remarked, what apparently he had not observed before, that there was something in my very countenance which indicated this: a dignity and benevolence which showed that I was, as he expressed it, "a divine man," an epithet which I suppose he would apply to a "marabout," or Moslem saint. I was glad to have his good opinion, however little I deserved it, and we parted with bowings and salaams that were not only kindly, but almost affectionate; and I shall always think of the simple old man as one of the really good Mussulmans on whom may descend the blessing of Allah and the Prophet!

From the Minister's we proceeded to the Palace of the Governor. Entering the court, we saw that we were to be received with some formality. In front of the arched entrance were drawn up a number of officials, who, the Consul explained, were not mere retainers of the palace, but "captains of the guard," who were called out only on special occasions and to do honor to exalted personages. They were stately figures in their long robes and snowy turbans. As we passed through this double line, Davis and I said not a word, but walked erect, stern and silent, as became our quite unknown (!) and mysterious importance, feeling the while that it was worth coming all the way from America to the Barbary coast to receive such homage.

At the grand portal the Governor met us to conduct us into the interior; and now, for the first time, we recognized a figure which answered to our ideal of a Moor. Davis, who is himself over six feet, had for once to look up, and whispered to me, as the Bashaw swept before us in his flowing robes, "What a magnificent specimen of manly strength and beauty!" He led us through a labyrinth of passages, coming out now and then into stately halls with exquisite points of architecture in ceilings and arches wrought in the Moorish fretted work, which is one of the beauties of the Alhambra.

But no one of these was the Hall of Audience, at least for us, but a sort of recess or alcove, into which the Governor took us, perhaps as a more familiar way of receiving those whom he counted his personal friends. Had we been Moslems, he would have seated himself in Moslem fashion, on a divan, or a broad mattress, covered with the gorgeous rugs of the East, where he would have doubled up his long legs under him. But in deference to our Christian customs, chairs had been placed for us. Nor would he sit in any other fashion himself. As there were only three chairs, we remained standing till he should take his seat; but, not to be outdone in courtesy, he insisted on my sitting down in the place reserved for him, while he stood till another chair was brought, and we were all seated together.

The Governor is much younger than the Minister, who is seventy, while he is but forty-two, and is much more a man of the world. He comes of a warlike race, one of his ancestors having fought against England when she held Tangier, and been among those who marched in when the English marched out. He is himself a general in the army, and carries himself like a soldier. Nor could a soldier of any country have been more gracious. And when coffee was brought in on a silver tray and served in tiny cups, after the dainty fashion of the East, we all felt the gentle stimulus, and the conversation grew animated, turning upon the affairs of the day, upon which the Governor showed himself well informed and talked intelligently.

But, while all this interested us, Davis and I, like true courtiers (or true editors), had come to court for an object. He, being somewhat of a sporting turn—that is, fond of riding, shooting, and hunting—was after big game; on the lookout to see something which others had not seen; and such a place there was in Tangier in the famous prison, which had a reputation almost as bad as the Black Hole of Calcutta, but into which no foreigner had been able to penetrate. Every stranger was taken to see the outside, but the only glimpse of what was within was through a hole in the wall, which was quite enough for most persons, who held their noses and their breath while they peered into the darkness of the interior. But we took it into our foolish heads that we should like to go farther. Nothing was too bad for our eyes to see or our stomachs to endure. But we were told that it was impossible. It was the common saying in Tangier, that "no one could go into the prison but prisoners." There was danger in the attempt. Some of the inmates had horrible diseases, and might give us the leprosy or the plague. Others were said to be raving maniacs, who might spring upon us and inflict some deadly injury before we could be rescued. And yet such is the perversity of human nature, that these dangers only stimulated our curiosity. So we ventured to ask, and even to urge, Colonel Mathews to obtain the desired permission. "You can manage it for us," I said. He promised to do what he could, but gave us no encouragement, for he had recently made the same request, and been politely, but firmly, refused. But, as the conversation with the Governor went on, and his heart seemed to warm toward us, I whispered to the Consul, "Now is your time." "Not quite yet," he answered, "wait a moment;" for he was too much of a diplomat to spoil the game by premature disclosure of his purpose, and he was skirmishing for position. Presently he leaned forward so that his head almost touched the Governor's, as if he had something to whisper confidentially, and made known our request. Instantly the Governor's countenance fell. He did not lose a particle of his courtesy, but he was in a predicament. For two years that he had been Governor, he had never given permission. If he yielded now, he would be importuned to do for others what he had done for us. All this the Consul admitted, but still asked it on the ground of personal friendship, which had the more weight, as he is a favorite with the Moorish officials, and when he added that it was a favor which he would not ask again, the Governor could no longer refuse; and as we rose to leave, he accompanied us to the outer court, and gave orders to an officer of the guard to go with us in person, and see that we were allowed to enter.

We had not far to go, for here, as in Venice, the palace and the prison are two parts of one institution. In the good old times, when the Kasbah was built, it was not merely as a royal residence, but as a citadel, with guns mounted on the outer wall; and it was convenient to have a place of punishment close at hand, so that one who fell under the Bashaw's displeasure could be instantly thrown into a dungeon. And so it is that the prison is in the courtyard of the palace, and, indeed, a part of it, and it is but a step from one to the other.

Colonel Mathews accompanied us to the entrance, but would not go inside. He had once been in as Consul, when he was recognized by the prisoners, who gathered round him, throwing themselves at his feet, seizing hold of his legs, kissing his hands, and beseeching him, in the name of God, to deliver them from their misery. He could hardly tear himself away, and had no wish to repeat the experiment. He saw us attempt it with some apprehension, and was relieved when we emerged in safety.

There are two prisons, side by side, one for the city and one for the country. We began with the former, to which there is no entrance but by a square window in the wall, which is closed up by a heavy door. This was swung open, and Davis sprang in and I followed; and when we heard it shut behind us with a bang, we knew that we were at last where we had wished to be, inside of the prison of Tangier.

To give my first impression, I was disappointed: it was not as bad as I had expected. To be sure, it was not an attractive place—prisons never are—but it was not a Chamber of Horrors. I saw no torture such as I had seen in China. In one respect it might be even more tolerable than the prisons of civilized countries, for at least the inmates had not solitude added to imprisonment. Instead of being shut up in cells, as in England and America, they were all in one large room, where, as misery loves company, they had whatever comfort could be found in such dreary companionship. They were spared, also, the vacancy and wretchedness of idleness; for, as they sat upon the ground, their fingers could be occupied in making out of palmetto grass the panniers that bestride the little donkeys of the city, by which they might earn a trifle for their own subsistence.

This would not be so bad, but the inhuman thing about it was, that the innocent were made to suffer with the guilty. There are no degrees of crime, and in some cases there may be no crime whatever; for men are thrown into prison for debt, for petty offences, or for none at all, but only as a means of extorting money for their release. Those who have done no wrong are forced into the vilest companionship, where all rot together in one foul mass of decaying humanity.

Here ended our first lesson, and we passed on to the next. The country prison, like the other, is bolted and barred in a way to show that it is not intended to be open to visitors. The only entrance is through a grated window, backed by a heavy wooden door, which was unlocked for us, and we climbed through the iron bars, throwing out our legs before us, so that we might fall on our feet. Here our field of observation was greatly increased, as this prison is very much larger than the other, and has in the centre a small court, with a space above it open to the sky for the admission of light and air. It has nearly three times as many inmates, with a greater variety of crime, the petty thieves of the city giving place to the bold brigands of the mountains, who have been the terror of the country, and made themselves famous by their crimes. In going into such a crowd the prison-keepers evidently felt that we were in some personal danger, for two of them followed us, and kept close at our heels, for fear of "accidents." But the precaution was hardly necessary, for the most desperate criminals were chained at the ankles, so that they could only hobble toward us. It was well that we met them here, rather than in some lonely place in the forest or on the desert, for I doubt not that more than one looked us in the eye who would kill a man as he would kill a sheep. These men were professional robbers and murderers, and scanned us from head to foot, in the way of business, trying to "size us up" in case they should have an opportunity to pay their respects to us under other conditions. But for the present they offered us no violence, nor made even a threatening gesture. They are pretty well subdued by the prison discipline, which is not by chains, nor flogging, nor the dark cell. There is something more effective than this, that will bring down the most hardened wretch that ever fought against society— it is starvation. This is the constant discipline in the prisons of Tangier, for there are no prison rations, no allowance of food whatever. He who gets it must pay for it like anybody else, and the few pence a day that he can earn, cannot go very far; and if his friends do not bring him something to eat, he must live on charity, a virtue that does not abound in Moslem countries. Hence they must often go for days without food, till they are on the borders of starvation. This cannot be carried beyond a certain point. It takes a strong man to stand it long. Many whom we saw were in the last stages. How frequent are the deaths we have no means of knowing, but we could not doubt that often, in the dead of night, naked bodies were taken out of that very window by which we crawled in, and dragged down the hill, to be thrown into a ditch or into the sea.

In the presence of such awful misery, one's moral reflections are silent. Whatever the crimes of these men, we could but feel the horrors of their situation. If they had raised a hand to strike us, we might strike back; but not so when the hand was stretched out with a look of anguish that seemed to say, "For God's sake, have pity on us!" My impulse was to take out a handful of small coin, and throw it right and left. But I was told that if I did this, the moment our backs were turned the poor creatures would fight among themselves for it, and the strongest would get it, leaving the weakest and most helpless worse off than before. Nor would it do to intrust money to buy bread to the keepers, who would put it in their pockets, and not a penny would ever reach the starving convicts, nor as much as a crust of bread be put into their hungry mouths.

I came away, saddened at what I saw, and sadder still that I could do nothing to relieve it. The scene haunted me. I had continually before me the picture of the men shut up within those walls, condemned to a living death. I saw the half-naked forms crouching upon the ground, trying to hide themselves under rags, cowering in the gloom, as Dante may have imagined the damned in the nethermost depths of hell.

When the blessed Sabbath came, I thought I would try to alleviate in some slight degree this physical suffering, if I could not drive away the mental horror and despair. If I could not trust the keepers of the prison to buy bread, I would go myself and buy it, and put it into the prisoners' hands. And so, taking a servant from the hotel, and a couple of soldiers from the Consul's, who could enforce my purpose with his authority, I sent them into the market with money to buy a hundred loaves of bread, and went on to the Kasbah to wait for their coming. In half an hour they appeared with a donkey bearing a load that was too heavy for the men to carry. The panniers were piled high with the loaves. But my work was not yet done. My major-domo said it would not do to leave the distribution to the keepers, for if I did, the greater part would never see the inside of the prison, but that I must go in myself, and put the bread into the prisoners' hands. So once more the grated windows opened, and, "accoutred as I was" in my Sunday dress, "I plunged in." Not to lose a single loaf, the men dragged in after me the very panniers that had been taken from the donkey's back, and spread them out on the prison floor, a sight, I venture to say, that these poor creatures never saw before. As there were over a hundred of them—thirty-two in the city prison and eighty-five in the other—there were not quite loaves to go round, so that some were broken in two; but half a loaf would be enough for "a square meal," or two or three such. Indeed, I believe it was more substantial food than many of them would get in a week. And never did I feel more grateful for any privilege than that of going from one to another, and giving to them bread with my own hands.

Some who are curious in their observation of human nature, even in its agonies, have asked how the prisoners received this unexpected visitation. Were they grateful for it? Did they show their gratitude? No, not much! A few rose up and came toward me, bewildered by the unexpected scene, but the greater part sat still upon the ground, like Job and his friends, in speechless misery. I was not disappointed at this silence, for I did not ask thanks for doing an act of humanity. Nor were they in a condition to be very demonstrative. When a man feels hunger gnawing at his vitals, his sensibility is deadened by his wretchedness. His misery makes him dumb. One, whose face was a little more human than the rest, beckoned to me, and to show that he could not move, lifted up his ragged covering, and exposed a body swollen with some horrible disease, and ready, like Judas, to burst asunder in the midst. I went to him and put a loaf into his hand, for which he murmured some words of thankfulness. There was an old man who sat on the floor by the entrance, whose eyes met mine, as I was coming out, with a peculiar expression. I stopped and took him by the hand, and gave him a double portion, and was glad to see him hide the loaves in his *jelab*, so that no one stronger than he could take them from him. He was content, and there stole over his face a faint appearance of Moslem resignation, which seemed to say, " It matters little, for it will soon be over."

Some may think, that having such an opportunity to preach to the spirits in prison, I should have improved the occasion to give them some good lessons. But I could speak to them only in the sign language; and even if I could have spoken in their own tongue, what could I say? Talk to them of God? They would answer, " There is no God, or He would not leave us in this misery." He who was wiser than we, fed the multitude as well as taught them. And for these poor creatures, who perhaps never received kindness before, it was better to wait till they recovered a little from the pangs of hunger, before attempting any instruction. So we left them to their own thoughts, to which the day's experience might give a new turn. I had some faith in the power of kindness. Perchance, I thought, when the night comes on, as they lie upon the ground and look upward through that open space in the roof to the firmament above them, the stars that shine so brightly in this eastern sky may not seem so far away, nor so cold and pitiless, and some faint recognition of a Higher Power may float upward to the throne of God.

CHAPTER VI

FROM TANGIER TO ALGIERS

TANGIER is not an easy place to get away from. A boat crosses the straits to Gibraltar two or three times a week, but it does not go up the Mediterranean. For that you must wait for the French boat from Cadiz, which makes a round trip, touching at different ports along the coast. It does not always suit the traveller's convenience, as now it did not suit mine, for it was to sail on the very day that the British Minister at Tangier was to give a reception, at which I should see the whole foreign colony, with officers from the other side of the straits, as the Governor of Gibraltar was coming over in a gunboat. The Bashaw, who is a real African lion, was to make his first appearance, with other "swell Moors," a mixture of European manners with barbaric splendor, that one would not miss seeing; but the steamer was to leave at noon, and if I did not go in her I should be detained another week.

But my friends would not have me depart unattended. The Consul insisted that I should go off under the American flag, and, with the Portuguese Minister, accompanied me to the ship, from which I looked up once more to the old Kasbah, leaving it with all its crimes upon its head. As we swept out of the bay and into the straits, Gibraltar soon looked down upon us, never bending his rocky head, but permitting us to pay our homage at his feet. However, I had two or three hours on shore, enough to see my old friend De Sauty, little thinking it was the last time (he died a few weeks after), and our Consul, Mr. Sprague, and the Rev. Mr. Murray, both of whom rode down with me to the landing to say good-by, so that I had two "send-offs" in one day.

When I was here before and took the same route, the next morning found us anchored at Malaga, where we spent a day, and the following day at Melilla, a penal settlement on the African coast, where the Spanish garrison has lately been attacked by the fierce native tribes. These Spanish ports are now omitted by the French steamer, which, on leaving Gibraltar, takes its course across the Mediterranean. The next morning found us off a rugged coast that rises up in places like the Palisades on the Hudson, and at longer distances like a mighty sea-wall, as if to defy the storms. To a landsman this long line of cliffs looks dangerous; one would not like to be caught in a northern gale that should dash a ship against this ironbound coast. But our French captain was a bluff old sea-dog, who was never quite at his ease except on his native element. He confessed to me that he never felt safe on land, and that if he were betrayed into putting his foot into a railway carriage he could not repress the feeling that he was in positive danger. But give him a stout bark, with ribs of oak, and a good copper bottom under him, and he was ready to venture into the most stormy sea, and give his ship and himself "to the lightning and the gale."

On these Mediterranean steamers one meets travellers of all countries. Walking the deck I recognized a face that I had seen in Tangier, in the company of a gentleman with whom I had a bowing acquaintance. That was quite enough for an introduction. I found that he was a Russian count, who, after the required years of service in the army, now gave himself to sport as the chief end of man, or as the chief delight of a soldier when he had not the greater excitement of war. In pursuit of this he had visited different parts of the world, shooting bears in America and lions in Africa. He told me how he went to Zanzibar and engaged a hundred and fifty men for an expedition into the interior. The greater part of these were simply bearers, carrying on their backs stores of every kind for the long march and for the camp. With these he started from the coast, and, crossing the jungle, pushed for the highlands, where, amid the boundless forests, he could find royal game. The lion had no terror for him, for he knew how to face the king of beasts. When he had struck the trail, and followed it up till he drew near the spot where the lion was concealed, he would not trust anybody but himself, for he knew that the first low growl would send the natives flying. So he kept them in the rear while he advanced alone, with his grip on the rifle that never failed him, never taking his eye off from one point, but reserving his fire till the great head rose up, with the glittering eyeballs looking straight at him. Then he raised his rifle—a flash, and the heavy ball sank into the lion's brain, and with one bound into the air he fell on the leaves of the forest.

With the same cool head and unshaken nerve he disposed of the elephant, though the skull was too thick to be penetrated by an ordinary musket ball. For elephant hunting, therefore, he had a four-barrelled rifle, with a bore so large that the discharge of them all was like firing grape and canister.

But to my inexperienced judgment it seemed as if the chance of being torn to pieces by a lion, or tossed on the tusk of an elephant, was not the only danger; there was one still greater in venturing alone with a hundred and fifty savages into the heart of an African forest. "How," I asked, "did you control your men?"

"Oh, that is easy when you have once shown them that you are their master! They soon found that I was not to be trifled with, but that, if they did their duty, they were well treated and had plenty to eat. That is a potent consideration with Africans, and at any sign of insubordination it was only necessary to cut off their rations to bring them to submission."

"But one of Stanley's lieutenants was killed by a native. Had you no fear of treachery? They might have killed you while you were asleep."

"I slept apart, and had one man who was devoted to me to keep watch, with orders to wake me instantly if he saw any one creeping toward my tent. That was enough. My rifle was always at hand, and would soon scatter them."

Sometimes severe measures were necessary. Where the fate of a whole expedition depends upon one man, he must be able to command absolute obedience, and he must not stop at anything to repress the first sign of mutiny. More than once he had hung a man in the sight of the whole camp. But, commonly, the rifle was better because it was quicker; he could level it the instant that he saw a threatening look.

"So," said the count, "the danger is not so great as it seems. The Africans are like children, and must be treated as such: not with cruelty on the one hand, nor indulgence on the other, but with firmness; when they soon learn to respect your authority, and follow you as the dog follows his master."

By this treatment the whole body, composed of such raw material, had been so disciplined that they followed him not sullenly, but with the utmost fidelity. Indeed, he had trained them to be soldiers, so that on more than one occasion they had stood firmly against the attacks of the warlike tribes through which he passed.

This was an exciting experience. I had read of such things in the narratives of Gordon Cumming and other mighty hunters. But it was another thing to have the story told by the actor in it, as we sat on the deck in the twilight, and glided along these African shores. But my companion had no idea of posing as a hero, and thought no more of shooting a lion than of smoking a cigar.

Other African scenes there were, the description of which kindled in me greater enthusiasm, such as that of his first sight of Ruwenzori, a mountain mass that is believed by many geographers to be none other than the ancient Mountains of the Moon, whose topmost peak, though lying under the equator, is covered with eternal snow; and of Kilimanjaro, of which Bayard Taylor wrote the majestic lines beginning:

> Hail to thee, monarch of African mountains!
> Remote, inaccessible, silent and lone—
> Who, from the heart of the tropical fervors,
> Liftest to heaven thine alien snows,
> Feeding forever the fountains that make thee
> Father of Nile and Creator of Egypt!

But while we are thus passing the hours, our good ship is speeding on her way. If there were no break in this ironbound coast, it would be unapproachable; but here and there Nature has kindly cleft it in twain, that man may enter. In one of these nooks, where boats can find shelter under the lea of a tremendous cliff, we made our first landing, at Nemours.

It is not "much of a place," and would not attract a moment's attention but for the fact that it is the first town in French territory; and that one word carries us, at a single bound, over the enormous abyss between barbarism and civilization. Here is a town laid out in the regular French style, presenting, if not a very imposing appearance, at least a respectable one, with a long row of warehouses facing the sea, the sign of commerce; and as soon as we set foot on shore, we find wide and well-paved streets, with wagons passing to and fro—a sight not to be seen in all Morocco. After three weeks in Tangier, where everything has to be transported on the backs of camels or donkeys or men, it was a novelty to see anything on wheels, if it were only a cart laden with military stores. Of course, in a frontier town the military element is conspicuous. The soldier is abroad, and the zouaves, with their red caps set jauntily on their heads, and their baggy Turkish trousers, make the streets and squares quite gay. A company was just marching out of one of the gates to practise firing at a target. It was good to find myself under the French flag, a sign that we had reached a land where we were under the protection of law supported by military power. But it is not merely soldiers that one sees in Nemours: there are schools for children, as well as barracks for troops; houses fit for human beings to live in, with everything that man needs that he may be clothed and warmed and fed; a hospital for the sick, and a church for the worship of God. All these were the signs that we had left behind us African barbarism, and entered once more into the sphere of European civilization.

Another night's sail brought us to Oran, which is a large seaport, in spite of the fact that the bay is so broad and open that a storm from the north would roll the waves into it with tremendous power. But this danger is guarded against by a long and massive breakwater, behind which the great steamers of the Compagnie Générale Transatlantique lie in safety.

We landed in the early morning. The town has somewhat of the picturesqueness of Tangier, a semi-circle of hills rising from the sea, and it has what Tangier has not, a decent government. At the very landing one sees the contrast between civilization and barbarism. Instead of being taken off the ship in a boat, by Arabs yelling and almost fighting over the possession of an unfortunate traveller, the steamer comes up to the quay, and the American aboard walks quietly on shore as at New York, and with less difficulty through the Custom House, which is an affair of five minutes; and then if he is eager to press on, he can at once depart for Algiers.

But Oran itself is well worth a day or two. Here is a city of seventy thousand inhabitants, in which there is a curious mixture of the Orient and Occident; of mosques and churches; French shops and Eastern bazaars. Wherever the French plant their foot, they make a little Paris; and, better still, their rule shows itself in a vigorous police, in the good order which is kept in the streets, and in the general European air of this African city.

The greatest surprise to the traveller who has just left Morocco will be when he drives to the station and takes his seat in a luxurious carriage for Algiers. A railroad in Africa! which we have been wont to think of as a land of deserts, to be traversed only by slow-moving caravans. In my boyish days I read the travels of Mungo Park, and was particularly moved by the incident of his coming, on one occasion, to an African village, and sitting down, footsore and weary, under a tree, where the natives saw him, but passed him with utter neglect, till some women came and invited him to their hut, and gave him food; and when he had lain down on the matting, he heard them singing:

> "The white man came and sat under a tree;
> The wind roared and the rain fell;
> Pity the poor white man!
> He has no wife to bring him milk,
> No wife to grind his corn."

Perhaps Mungo Park fell asleep listening to that song, and dreamed a dream of the future of the Dark Continent; but in his wildest dream was never a vision so utterly beyond belief in his waking hours as that the day would come when travellers would be whirled in fire-drawn cars along the shores and over the mountains of Africa.

It is a long day's ride from Oran to Algiers. It would not be long in France or America, for the distance is but four hundred and twenty kilometres (about two hundred and fifty miles), or as far as from New York to Boston, or to Washington, over which one of our fast trains would pass in six hours. But here they make a full day of it, starting at ten in the morning and arriving at ten at night. There is some excuse for this slowness, for the country is new; and as there is but one through train a day, it must needs stop at every little French settlement. Impatient Americans may think this very tedious. But I found the day full of interest, as I was in no haste to reach a destined point, but only wished to see the country. As the count and I had a compartment to ourselves, we had the utmost freedom of conversation, and when Africa grew dull, could change the subject, and talk of Russia or America. But Africa did not grow dull. As we were all the time looking out of the windows, there was always something new to observe.

On leaving Oran we bore away from the sea, of which we did not have a glimpse again till we approached Algiers. The country was at first uncultivated. A few Arabs here and there were tending their flocks, but for the most part the region seemed thinly inhabited, although the native population may be more considerable nearer the coast. But I was more interested in observing the beginning of French settlements. As we stopped at the stations, it was pleasant to see with what care the French emigrants were cultivating their plots of ground, surrounding their little houses with gardens, in which were orange trees and olive trees, and other fruit trees grown in a semi-tropical climate, while in a wider circle were vineyards (for the French seem to take by instinct to the cultivation of the vine), and fields of wheat and barley. I observed along the route what I thought were haystacks, but was told that they were not for the food of cattle, but for the service of man in another way, being stacks of a kind of grass which is used as a material for making paper, and has become an important article of commerce. Do you say that all this put together does not amount to much? But these are the beginnings of civilization. These scattered farmhouses will be so many centres for French emigrants, around which will cluster more and more thatch-roofed cottages, till the hamlet has become a village, and the Province of Oran will be a reproduction of what one sees in the less-peopled parts of Normandy or Brittany.

One thing struck me by its absence: there were no great forests, which I ascribed to the wastefulness of the Arab population, for nature has interposed no obstacle to their growth. The soil is rich and the climate propitious. There is nothing in the heat of Africa that should cause vegetation to shrink and wither. On the contrary, perhaps the world does not show, unless it be in the valley of the Amazon, a greater forest than that of the Aruwimi, which Stanley describes. Here, too, there might be the same illimitable wilds. There are numerous cedar forests in other parts of Algeria; they grow on the Aures Mountains as on Mount Lebanon: why should the seacoast be stripped and bare? I can ascribe it only to the wastefulness of the Arabs, who strip the country of its forests, to burn the wood for charcoal, with no attempt at replacing what they destroy. Since the French have come in they have made large plantations, so that another generation may see Algeria transformed into a well-wooded country; but, for the present, I did not see, in all this day's ride, a single forest, nor a single tree that would be a country's pride, like one of the great oaks of England, or one of the elms of America.

One sight we had, midway in our day's journey, that was very painful: the drying up of large tracts of country from the want of rain. The cloudless skies of Africa may excite the rapture of poets and travellers, but it is possible to have too much of a good thing; and just at this moment the prayer of the country is, that the windows of heaven may be opened and the floods descend. Already the Arabs have no grazing for their sheep, that are likely to perish by thousands, while the people themselves are reduced almost to the point of starvation, so that collections are being taken up in all the cities for their relief.

But in the afternoon the country was less desolate, and the scene increased in beauty as we travelled farther to the east. On our right rose the long chain of the Atlas Mountains, which, as the sun sank behind us, took lights and shadows that made us sit silent, gazing at the magnificent spectacle. In such a soft and tender light the evening drew on, but it was ten o'clock when our train swept round the curve of a beautiful bay, across which we saw in the distance long rows of lights, and soon rolled into the station at Algiers. As I stepped from the carriage, a friendly face looked into mine, and the American Consul took me by the hand, and led the way to the hotel, where I soon found myself perched in an airy room, with a balcony from which I looked down into a square full of palms.

CHAPTER VII

ALGIERS

This African journey is full of surprises in the sharp contrasts which give to each new place a *couleur locale* quite unlike that of its predecessor. One cannot imagine a greater change than that from Tangier to Algiers. They have hardly anything in common, except that they are both in Africa and both on the Mediterranean. But Algiers is a European city, while Tangier is distinctly African. And yet Tangier is much nearer Europe; indeed, it is in sight of it. From my windows I could look across to the shores of Spain. But for all that, I felt that I was out of the world. But here, though it is five hundred miles across the sea, we are in close touch with France and with all Europe. Every afternoon, at three o'clock, the steamer which left Marseilles the day before at noon, rounds into the bay; while the submarine telegraph reports the doings of the Chamber of Deputies, which appear in the morning papers as regularly, if not as fully, as in those of Paris itself.

As Algiers, or the French part of it, is the offspring of Paris, it is a true son of its father, whom it copies in all respects, in its very architecture, as in its way of life. More than one long colonnade is an exact reproduction of the Rue de Rivoli; the shops and restaurants and *cafés* are almost as gay as those on the banks of the Seine; and as one sees the great number of people sitting round the tables, sipping their coffee, and talking

A STREET IN THE OLD TOWN OF ALGIERS

as only Frenchmen can talk, he might easily imagine himself on the Boulevards.

But the beauty of Algiers is not in its likeness to Paris, but rather in its difference from it, by reason of its latitude, which gives it another climate, so that in two days one passes from bleak winter to a land where the seasons are rolled backward—or forward—giving perpetual spring. The charm is not in the city itself, but in its atmosphere, in the balmy air, in the palms and the flowers that bloom in midwinter; and in its surroundings, the encircling hills, crested with villas, from whose broad verandas look out, not eastern houris, but noble English and American women, who in this land of the sun gather in their interiors all the attractions of their distant homes.

With such a climate it is not strange that the English in great numbers leave their island, wrapt in fog and mist, and seek a winter home on the southern shores of the Mediterranean. I meet them everywhere—in the hotels, in the streets, and on all the country roads, driving or riding on horseback, while in the suburb of Mustapha Superieur the residences are largely those of the English colony. The most beautiful point of all is that occupied by the British Consul-General, Sir Lambert Playfair, whose house is naturally the rallying place of those whom he so worthily represents, and at whose weekly receptions one is sure to meet all that is most distinguished among his countrymen and country-women.*

---

* " Lieut.-Col. Sir R. Lambert Playfair, K.C.M.G.—*Par nobile fratrum*—one of a family of soldiers and savants, is a name very familiar to all African travellers. As Political Resident at Aden and Zanzibar, it was his lot to see the coming and going of many of the most famous

To me Algiers is encircled with a double halo, as I have been here before, and the impressions of the two visits meet and mingle. If I should once or twice allude to what I saw six years ago, it is because the memory is very grateful to me; and there is a sweetness in the air as I recall scenes and persons which, though past and gone, are still cherished and beloved. One figure that I saw then I miss now, that of Sir Peter Coats, to whom I brought a letter from Mr. Junius S. Morgan of London. Sir Peter was a grand specimen of the Scotchman of the olden time, whose "good gray head all men knew." His simplicity and kindness reminded me of our Peter Cooper, whom he resembled also in the union of wealth and benevolence, which had made his name as familiar to the public of Great Britain as is that of our philanthropist to the people of America. After a long life devoted to active pursuits, he felt, as he approached his eightieth year, that he was not sufficiently rugged to bear the winter of his native Scotland, and so he migrated like the birds, and took refuge in Algiers, where he had a villa high up on the hillside, which looked off upon one of the most enchanting scenes in the world. In this hospitable home I was always welcome, and often his

---

explorers, to send them forth on their missions, and to welcome them when they returned to these 'jumping-off places' of a then little continent. At a later date—from the year 1867—as Consul-General for Algeria, and for a time for Tunisia also, Sir Lambert has not only been the guide and friend of the many thousands of his countrymen who seek health in the French colony, but by his long journeys through the vast region with which he is, or has been, officially connected, and his many works, reports, and papers descriptive of it, he takes a high place among those who have shed light on the dark places of Northern Africa."—From "The Story of Africa," by the well-known geographer, Dr. Robert Brown. Published by Cassell, London.

carriage was at the door of my hotel to have me accompany him in his drives over the hills.

In one of these he took me to call at a Mr. Macleay's, whose surroundings may show how these wanderers from Britain contrive to make themselves comfortable during the days of their absence. We found him in the centre of a large estate, some hundreds of acres, in what had once been a Moorish palace. Though three hundred years old, its walls were still strong, and, finding no occasion to tear it down, he reconstructed it in accordance with his English ideas, having apparently no end of means to carry out every desire of his artistic taste. Some alterations were necessary to fit it for the use of an English family, its last occupant having been a rich Kabyle, whose large household required apartments that were not needed for the present owner's English, or, rather, American wife, a lady from Boston. In the arrangements of the interior there was a mingling of that which recalled the East with that which recalled the West. The Oriental architecture was preserved, the Moorish arches and the fretted work, delicate as lace, and which looked as if it would be equally soft to the touch; and at the same time the blank spaces on the walls were hung with pictures, and the marble pavements covered with Turkish or Persian rugs; while the books and periodicals on the tables gave to the place the air of an English gentleman's library. In one of the rooms an open fire was blazing on the hearth, even while the doors were swung wide, and palms were growing in the open air. The court, which always forms the centre of a Moorish house, was like a conservatory for flowers, and here the gracious mistress of the place gave us a truly English-American welcome, setting before us (as it was the hour of afternoon tea) the cup which is at once so fragrant and delicious. Thus, in a Moorish palace we found the comfort, as well as the taste and refinement, of an English home. With such an illustration, we had to confess that if, for reasons of health, Britons were banished from their native island, they had compensations to mitigate the pains of exile.

Compared with this large English colony the American element is small. But there are always some of our countrymen coming and going, whose faces it is pleasant to see. As the readiest way of being brought in contact with these birds of passage, no one should forget to call on our Consul, Mr. C. T. Grellet, a gentleman who, as his name implies, is of French descent, though born in California, where his father was among the "Forty-Niners," though he soon returned to France, from which he removed to Algeria. Thus France and America are united in the person of father and son, and the latter is most happily fitted by birth and education to be a connecting link between the two great Republics of Europe and America.

To Mr. Grellet I owe my first introduction to Algiers. He went with me everywhere. One day he drove me out to Koubba, to pay a visit to his father, a fine old gentleman, who has long been a resident of the country. As it was Friday (the Mohammedan Sunday), the Arab population were going to their cemetery. It seemed a strange union of seclusion and publicity to see women, closely veiled in the Eastern fashion, riding in an omnibus. Around the entrance to the cemetery they were gathered in great numbers. No strangers are admitted on that day. This weekly visit would be, like the *Jour des Morts* in Paris, very touching, were it not that they convert it into a kind of picnic, spreading out their clothes on the ground, and taking their refreshment, which is enlivened by the incessant chatter of Arab women; and the merry laugh goes round, unchecked by the solemn presence of the dead.

A little farther we met an Arab funeral. The body, uncoffined, but simply stretched on a litter and covered with a cloth, was carried by bearers, who were constantly relieved by others who pressed forward to take the sacred burden. Perhaps a hundred persons followed, to the music of a mournful chant. The burial has no feature of solemnity. There is no service of committal to the grave : indeed, there is no committal at all; the uncoffined dead being merely shoved into a kind of oven of brick, and left to moulder in utter forgetfulness. It is different with the burial of a marabout, whose sanctity makes his tomb a shrine for the resort of pilgrims.

As we swept along the road, a more beautiful sight came into view in the Jardin d'Essai, which was begun as a Jardin d'Acclimatation, for the naturalization of plants of other countries and climates, where one may walk under avenues of bamboos, magnolias, and palms.

As we began to mount the hills, there opened before us, on every side, a view of exquisite beauty. Behind us was Algiers, one mass of white walls, that glittered in the sun, as they were set against a background of hills, with the bay in front, while on the horizon stretched the blue Mediterranean. Farther to the south was the chain of the Atlas Mountains, covered with snow. Mounting still higher, we were on the top of the Sahel, and our view turned in another direction—over into a broad and fertile valley, the Metidja, which divides the Sahel from the lower slopes of the Atlas.

Driving up to the house of Mr. Grellet, senior, he came out to meet us, and gave me a hearty welcome. Though by birth a Frenchman, he has lived both in North and South America, in New York, in Chili, and in California, where he has left his heart, for he thinks it the best of all lands. I was happy to tell him that the country round him, in its graceful undulations, and especially in the feature of a broad valley hemmed in by mountains, reminded me of Southern California. The reason of his frequent change of country was health. Not finding it in America, he returned to France, but found no relief till he crossed the Mediterranean and settled in Algeria twenty-five years ago, where he has remained to this day; and, though he is now seventy-two, he is as hale and hearty a man as one would wish to see, and bids fair to enjoy life for years to come.

Like many of his countrymen who came hither at an early day, he has devoted himself to the cultivation of the vine, and he took us out to see his vineyard. The grapes are pressed by machinery—he paying no heed to the fancy of the old time that the wine is better if the grapes are pressed by the foot. By the machinery every drop is expressed, and then the very dregs cut up, and, as we should say, "mashed" and pressed again; and from this residuum is distilled the spirit that is put into the wine to keep it, so that there is no ingredient in the finished product but that which is of the grape itself.

The place for pressing the grapes and storing the wine is in the lowest ground on the estate, for the sake of coolness, for which reason the casks are often placed in cellars. In this case the *cave* is a building I should say a hundred—perhaps a hundred and fifty—feet long and two stories high, with enormous *tonneaux* for receiving the blood of the grape from the press, and keeping it till it is fermented, and works itself clear, when it is drawn off into barrels or casks for exportation.

From this exhibition of French industry we drove off in another direction from that by which we came, over the hills and through the valleys, making a circuit which took in every variety of landscape.

On another excursion Mr. Grellet took me to the old town of Algiers, which is a curiosity shop—a labyrinth through which few strangers wind from end to end so as to see anything of the interior life of the place. Their guides take them through the streets, but they see only the outside of the houses. As one climbs up the hill, he finds the street so narrow that a donkey loaded with panniers crowds him to the wall, and he declares Old Algiers to be a mere rabbit warren, in which human creatures burrow, as animals burrow under ground. But all who have travelled in the East know that in most Oriental houses there is not only an absence of show on the outside, but an ostentatious plainness, and even a look of poverty, so as not to attract the rapacity of the government; while there may be not only comfort, but luxury, within. So here a blank wall facing the street may hide a cheerful interior. Sir Lambert Playfair tells me that if I would stoop low enough (I suppose I should have to to bend my stiff American neck) to enter the humble door, I should presently come into a court open to the sky, and find that, as the houses in Algiers are built on a hillside, and rise one above another, these inner courts are bright, sunny, and airy; while the occupants have an outlook over the town below, and beyond over land and sea.

One glimpse I caught of something bright in a peep

into an Arab school, whose small quarters opened on the street, where a dozen children, leaving their sandals at the door, were sitting at their low desks, taking their lessons from the Koran, but not without furtive glances at the strangers who passed, with an expression which showed that they were by no means wanting in intelligence.

The Arab children are always bright. In my first walk about the town I was captured by the bootblacks, little fellows who have all the cunning of their tribe as seen in European and American cities. To their sharp eyes a foreigner is an object of special attraction, and, as there is a lively competition for "business," no sooner does he show himself in the street than they set off in pursuit; and as they run swiftly with their bare feet, they soon bring him down. It did not take them long to make a captive of me. Who would not surrender, with two of these little chaps holding him fast by his legs? I did not beg for mercy, but only asked for a chair to sit upon; and then, dividing myself, gave them a leg apiece, and was soon "polished off," so that I looked "quite respectable," at least till I should reach the next corner, when, if a passing carriage should throw a speck of dirt on my shining boots, it would be necessary to repeat the operation. The pay for this service is one whole penny (two sous), which will buy the little Arab enough bread to last for the day; and when I gave them a double portion, they were elated, while their companions looked on with envy. From that moment I was well known to the whole tribe, who spotted me as a "soft one;" and whenever they saw me coming round the corner, or sauntering along the boulevard that looks off upon the quay, they set after me in full cry. I think I never purchased so much pleasure at so slight a cost.

AN ARAB SCHOOL

CHAPTER VIII

THE ROBBERS' DEN

It is so bewitching to saunter about the streets in this African sunshine, that one is apt to forget that Algiers was not always so attractive to European visitors. For three hundred years it was in the power of the Infidel, who ruled with an iron hand. The only Christians to be seen were at work in the galleys, or at some other kind of hard labor, or in the servants' halls of great houses, always in some menial occupation. If they had any skill as artificers, it was put to use in the decoration of the houses of their masters. All the old palaces of Algiers, among which are those of the Governor and Archbishop, are filled with elaborate carvings in wood and stone, miracles of labor, which must have required the toil of years, all of which was the work of Christian slaves.

Nor is it so long since this high carnival of barbarism had sway, for it continued till within the memory of men now living. It is only sixty-three years ago that the flag of the Moslem floated from the Kasbah on yonder hill!

A place of such grim associations is worth a visit. It is a pretty steep climb, but not wearisome if taken in the afternoon, when that side of the hill is in shadow, and if you make frequent pauses by the way, as you will, to turn and look down upon the city at your feet, or off upon the Mediterranean. Here is an open space that you might pass without notice, if not told that it is the place where the guillotine is set up for capital offenders. A gruesome spot, indeed, but not unworthy of being kept in view among a turbulent and lawless people. Thus slowly climbing higher and higher, you reach the top, when a glorious outlook bursts upon the sight. Here stood the old castle, now dismantled and gone. But what a history it has to make men shudder! For this was the greatest den of robbers in the world, as it was the stronghold of the Barbary pirates, who, from this headland height, kept a sharp lookout north, east, and west, for any sail that might show itself on the horizon. For three centuries they preyed on the commerce of all nations. Not only did they rob ships of their cargoes, but the unhappy voyagers were seized as lawful prey, to be subjected to the most cruel slavery.

The horrors endured by these wretched "prisoners and captives" is almost beyond belief. The story has been told by Sir Lambert Playfair, in his "Scourge of Christendom," one of the most thrilling tales of suffering in the annals of mankind, yet not without relief in the courage with which it was borne, and the friendship and devotion which it called forth. Cases were not wanting of those who became so bound together by their common suffering, that when one was ransomed by his kindred at home, he would not accept deliverance, refusing to leave his friend behind. And to the eternal honor of the Roman Catholic Church be it remembered that priests volunteered to go among their brethren in captivity, even though they must needs be themselves enslaved, so that they might give to others the consolations of religion! But that such a state of things should be continued at all in the nineteenth century was the disgrace of the civilized world. True, the danger of personal capture and slavery was somewhat reduced by the payment of tribute to the Barbary powers—a tribute that was paid by almost, if not quite, every European state—but this was itself a confession of weakness or want of courage that was to the shame of all Christendom! Our own country, too, paid for a time, but it had the excuse of being the most helpless in the case, because the farthest away. And to its honor, be it said, it was the first power to refuse to pay it longer. In 1815 the United States sent Commodore Decatur to "serve notice" on the Dey of Algiers that from that time forth we should pay tribute no more. The Dey, seeing that the American captain was in earnest, and fearing the effect of such an example, tried to compromise, and modestly suggested that he would accept even a little powder, just to keep up appearances, to which the gallant Commodore replied that "if he took the powder, he must take the balls too!" a suggestion which was not at all agreeable; and the Dey soon made the best of a bad case by yielding the point, virtually admitting that rather than receive that kind of tribute, he would receive none at all. But this was a mere prologue to the great drama that was now opening, the chief act in which was performed the following year, when an English fleet under Lord Exmouth anchored off the mole, and laid half of the city in ruins.

Algiers was then at the mercy of England, and some may think it a want of foresight that, having possession, she did not do what France did afterwards, keep it, as she has kept other parts of the world, as an inseparable portion of the mighty British Empire. But this great inheritance was to go to the country of St. Louis, who, nearly six centuries before, had led a crusade to Jerusalem for the rescue of the Holy Sepulchre. To France it remained to give the *coup de grace* to this relic of barbarism. It came about in a somewhat dramatic way. The relations of the two powers had long been strained, but with no rupture, till in a conference between the Dey of Algiers and the representative of France, the former so far forgot himself as to strike the latter in the face with his fan! That settled him—not the Frenchman who received the blow, but the barbarian who gave it. The offence was worse than a defeat, for every man in France felt as if he had been struck in the face—an insult that could only be washed out in blood. It is one of the most remarkable cases in history, to illustrate the fact that great events may follow from small causes, that a *coup d'éventail* led to the overthrow of a kingdom! In 1830 the French landed an army, with orders to settle the business once for all. The haughty Algerines, who, from the immunity they had enjoyed in centuries of crime, had come to feel sure of the protection of Allah, were somewhat shaken in their minds as the bombs began to fly over their city and to crash through the roofs of the houses. When at last they were compelled to submit, and were spared the further horrors of bombardment, it was upon the inexorable condition that they surrendered their power forever!

And so the old flag that had floated over the Kasbah for centuries came down, and the new flag went up, and is floating there to-day. Never was there a greater victory of civilization over barbarism. It was not merely a revolution: it was an earthquake; as when in nature there is an upheaval of the solid earth so complete that the position of the different strata is exactly reversed, so that what was below is above, and what was above is below. The Arab could not understand it; he was deprived of his natural right to oppress all who were not true believers. Men whom he had despised before, who had to get out of his way as he walked the street, now stood erect, calling no man master. How these relations were changed the following will show: Standing one day in the street with the American Consul, two Jews passed, men of good presence, portly and well preserved, with blue turbans on their heads, and costly robes flowing to their feet. Observing the air of conscious dignity which they wore, my friend remarked that there was a time, and that not so very long ago, when they could not have carried their heads so high. Then no Jew could ride on horseback; he must ride on a donkey. If he approached a Moor, he must stoop and kiss his feet, or make such other profound obeisance as should be an acknowledgment of his own inferiority. Well, well! Those good old times are gone, and, in spite of Allah and the Prophet, they will not return.

But it is easier to conquer than to govern, and I sometimes hear doubts expressed as to the success of the experiment which the French are now making on so large a scale in Africa. "No doubt it is very fine for the French to be masters of an empire in Africa; but," says an American friend, in the slang of his country, "haven't they got rather a big job on their hands?" Yes, no doubt. The business of government is never a light affair; it is always a burden and a responsibility. It is difficult enough to govern one's own country; much more to govern a people of another race, inflamed with bitter animosity, and who have many facilities for defence in flying to the desert or the mountains.

The hatred of race is intensified by difference of religion. It is not a rule over Christians, but over Moslems, with whom old laws and customs, founded on the Koran, have acquired the force of nature and the sacredness of religion. Nowhere is it more necessary to "walk softly," for there is a sleeping devil in every native; and these old bearded Arabs, who seem very dull and slumberous as they sit cross-legged and motionless, smoking their long pipes, may be roused, by appeal to race hatred and religious fanaticism, to a holy war. The population is composed of elements in which there is constant danger. As it is divided into tribes, each with a sheik at its head, these may easily be converted into so many military organizations. Here is a magazine of gunpowder that may be exploded by the touch of a fanatic.

But the greater the difficulty, the greater the skill of the statesman who can not only subdue, but conciliate, an adverse population; and this, I think, the French have done here in a degree that shows a genius for government as marked, if not shown on so grand a scale, as that of the British in India.

When I came to Algiers six years since, I came by way of Spain, and in Madrid met the French Ambassador,* who had just come from Africa, where he had been the Resident of Tunis, and he talked freely about the political situation, telling me how he had conciliated the good will of the natives by a scrupulous respect to their customs, and, above all, to their religious observances. He did not allow a European to put his foot in a mosque. In this he followed out the policy of the French Government, which holds, or professes to hold, a

---

* M. Cambon, now Ambassdor in Turkey, and brother of the present Governor of Algeria.

position of absolute neutrality between all faiths, even going so far as to support those who officiate in the mosques, on the principle of supporting all forms of religious worship; maintaining Protestant pastors and Jewish rabbis, as well as Catholic priests.

When I left Madrid he gave me a letter to M. Tirman, then Governor of Algeria, on whom I called to pay my respects. For a long time after the French took possession of the country, it had been the custom to choose a soldier for governor, with the idea that he might have military duties to perform. The place had been held by Marshal de MacMahon, and by the Duke d'Aumale, and I expected to see a marshal of France in the governor's palace, or at least an officer of high rank; and was a little surprised, when introduced into his private cabinet, to find a very quiet gentleman, absorbed in the details of his extensive and difficult administration. He was extremely courteous, and gave me a hearty welcome to the country, offering me any service in his power to render my visit a pleasant one. I had no service to ask, but was glad of the opportunity of seeing the man who held a position in Africa with more power than the Khedive of Egypt.

He told me that the country over which he ruled was nearly as large as France; and even though half of it were desert, yet the half which was not desert, and parts of which were extremely fertile, would make a number of French provinces. It contained a population of three and a half millions, to govern which was far more difficult than to govern an equal number in France itself, where there was a homogeneous population. He had been governor for six years, and had thus had opportunity to become well acquainted with the country and the people. He did not conceal from himself the difficulty of French rule in Africa. But the very caution with which he spoke, the clearness with which he stated the difficulties, and the means by which they were to be met, seemed to furnish the best proof that he was well prepared for a position of such vast responsibility.

As the danger to the French rule lies in the division of the people into tribes, each with its own head forming an *imperium in imperio*, it is the policy of the Government to limit the authority of the sheiks, not by directly displacing them, but by relieving them of the cares of government in certain districts, which are turned over to French *administrateurs*. This neutralizes the power of the native chiefs, and removes one great danger to the French Government in Africa.

To disarm still further the hostility of the native population, many of the most athletic young men in the tribes, such as might be leaders in a rebellion, are enlisted in the army, not in regiments of the line, but as special troops for special duty, of which the Tirailleurs Indigènes, or Turcos, are infantry; while the Spahis form a body of irregular cavalry. Both are very picturesque, and I doubt not would make good soldiers in the field. The Spahis, especially, are what may be called a natural product of the desert. They may almost be said to have been born in the saddle, accustomed as they are from early boyhood to the wild riding of the plains, which makes them as much at home on horseback as the Cossacks of Russia or our American Indians. When they visit Paris, crowds rush to the Champ de Mars to witness their magnificent horsemanship. Of course they make splendid cavalry.

But this training of so many thousands of natives to arms would be in itself a new danger, were not the greatest precautions taken that the skill and power thus attained should not be turned on the wrong side. To this end all the officers of rank are French; and as they keep in their hands the arsenals, together with the strong fortresses in the mountains, the danger of insurrection, if not entirely removed, is very greatly reduced.

But no government is strong that relies on mere brute force. Force must be tempered with wisdom. In the exercise of power over races that are jealous and suspicious, there is need of all the French tact and courtesy. The iron hand is none the less firm for being hidden in a velvet glove. Absolute justice to the native population will make them recognize the advantage to themselves of a government under which they are free, and which yet is strong enough to give them perfect protection. Law founded in justice, and enforced by power, will conquer the world.

CHAPTER IX

IN GRAND KABYLIA

Of the travellers who cross the Mediterranean, the greater part make the city of Algiers the beginning and end of their journey in Africa; whereas it ought to be neither the beginning nor end, but only the middle. He who comes from Tangier and Oran has seen much; but he who keeps on to Constantine and Tunis will see more. Indeed, it is not until one has passed Algiers, on his way to the East, that he sees what is most grand in African scenery. In coming from Oran we saw mountains, but only at a distance; but now we are to be among them, as in passing through Switzerland we are among the Alps.

It was in the early morning, while the stars were still shining, that we glided out from under the terrace at Algiers, passing over the same route by which we had come, for there is but one railway approach to the city. As we swept round the bay, I kept watch, from the window, of the long line of lights, that seemed as if they were but a reflection of the stars above in the waters below. It was not till we were quite out of the city that we came to the parting of the ways, and turned eastward. Though it was not yet day, the light was beginning to show itself on the horizon, and at length the sun rose without a cloud—the sun of Africa—as if to welcome us to another part of his dominions.

In leaving Algiers, as in leaving Oran, we soon take

leave of the sea. A passage along the coast would be
obstructed by the mass of mountains. As it is, we shall
have to pierce them at many points, always seeking, of
course, the lowest level, but still checked and baffled by
projecting spurs, in compassing which, if we cannot
climb over them, we shall be obliged to wind round
them, or to creep under them by the innumerable tunnels
we shall enter before the day is over.

After two or three hours we enter a hill country,
where the French settlements are less frequent than
nearer the coast. And yet, sometimes, as we mount a
summit, we look down into a deep valley where a little
hamlet nestles under a rustic church, and in the shadow
of the church is a cemetery (how lonely it seems in the
mountains!) in which the crosses at the head of the
humble graves show that those who died here, far from
their beloved France, received Christian burial.

Another hour and we have mounted higher still, from
the hills to the mountains, till we are suddenly plunged
into a gorge that would be notable in Switzerland or in
the Rocky Mountains. This is the gorge of Palæstro,
where the mountains are cut in twain by a river that
rushes and roars, far below us, over its rocky bed.

To cut a passage through this rugged country was a
work of enormous difficulty, but it was a military necessity if the French were to keep possession of the country.
If they were to remain masters of Algeria, they must
hold the passes of the mountains, the home of a people
who had shown, in 1871, how formidable they might be.
To overawe these mountain warriors, the French must
be able to get at them; and for this purpose they built
a macadamized road through this gorge, and over the
mountains, which is as perfect in its construction as that

which the first Napoleon built over the Simplon. And now that magnificent highway is supplemented by an iron road, which seems to have been built with as little regard to cost as if it had been in the most densely populated part of France. Like a road in the Alps, it had to be guarded, if not against avalanches, at least against the melting of snow, which sets in motion floods that pour down the mountains with such fury as to sweep away all but the most solidly constructed works of man. The bridges had to be carried at a great height, sometimes a hundred feet above the chasms below. But they seem to have taken precautions against all dangers. The bridges are of iron, which opposes less surface to the rush of waters than massive arches of stone. For long distances the road is supported by enormous embankments, and where there is no projecting rock or earth for these to stand on, tunnels are cut through the heart of the mountains.

All this indicates that the French in Algeria have come to stay. The only drawback to this is not physical, but moral; it is in the French themselves, who, if they submit for a time to expatriation, are always sighing for *la patrie*.

At Palæstro there entered the railway compartment a Frenchman and his wife, who, instead of taking seats, remained standing, looking out of the window on one side and the other. I soon discovered that he was the engineer to whom had been entrusted the building of the bridges which I had been admiring, and I paid him compliments on his splendid work, expressing the hope that he would live to see all these mountain valleys filled by a French population; to which Madame quickly replied, "But we hope to return to France." "Ah, yes," said the husband, "there is but one France." It is this longing for the old home that makes it difficult for the French to become good colonists. But, in spite of all this, the line of the railroad is bordered by a number of villages, peopled by emigrants from Alsace and Lorraine, who, driven from their own homes by the German possession of the Rhine, can here sing the Marseillaise amid the mountains of Africa.

But the country before us soon engages our attention. The gorge of Palæstro marks a geographical division, the ridge of the mountain which overhangs it being the dividing line between the Arabs and the Kabyles. On the western side are the Arabs, while on the eastern, which we are entering, are the Kabyles, so that we are now in Grand Kabylia, the Switzerland of Africa. True, the mountains are not so high as the Alps, but they are like them in that, instead of forming a continuous chain, like the Pyrenees or Apennines, they stand apart, as separate peaks, whose conical shape indicates that they are old volcanoes, whose fires burned out long ago, and over which have grown great forests, while the "wild torrents, fiercely glad," pour down the mountain sides; and if there be nothing to equal the Matterhorn or the Jungfrau, there is yet many a wild pass and rugged height to tempt the Alpine climber.

If it will give an additional zest to his mountaineering to carry a gun, he may find an abundance of game to exercise his skill. An old French officer, who came into our compartment, told me that a daring hunter may, or might, not long ago, have had a chance of shooting a panther (or leopard); or even, now and then, of stirring up an African lion! Of course, the advance of civilization drives the king of beasts farther back into the recesses of the mountains; and yet a Hungarian gentleman, who was a fellow-traveller, told me that, even since the Franco-Prussian war, two of his cousins spent three months here in Kabylia, in company with the famous Jules Gérard, hunting lions. This royal game has nearly disappeared since the Government offered a reward for every lion that was killed; but there are still panthers, which sometimes come about the villages, and snap up the dogs. Nor need the most adventurous huntsman despise this as inferior game, for, said my informant, " the panthers grow to enormous size; some have been shot, measuring almost as long as tigers."

In default of lions or panthers, an ordinary sportsman may have to content himself with shooting or spearing wild boars. Monkeys, too, are here in great numbers. " Do you see that mountain yonder?" said the officer, pointing to a peak in the distance, " it is given up to the monkeys: they may almost be said to be its only inhabitants; the woods are full of them!" But to shoot them would be almost a massacre of the innocents, or of the lower members of the human family. " Pray, do not," says a friend, " encourage the slaughter of our far-away cousins!"

But more interesting than boars and monkeys, or even panthers or lions, are the people who inhabit these mountains. The Kabyles are quite different from the Arabs —different in origin, in features, and in language. The Arabs are comparatively new-comers, having come into Northern Africa with the Moslem invasion, while the Kabyles are supposed to be the descendants of the ancient Mauritanians, who were here before the Romans, and even before the Carthaginians. With all the mixtures of foreign blood, they still show the peculiarities of their race. The Arabs are taller and more slender; more wiry and nervous; the Kabyles are shorter and "stockier," better suited to hard labor.

The Kabyles are a very warlike people, a character which they inherit from their ancestors. There seems to be a fitness of things, a correspondence to nature, in that a wild and savage country, long the habitation of lions, should be also the home of a people as brave as lions, who from time immemorial have fought for their independence. When the Romans, after destroying Carthage, pursued their conquests westward, along Northern Africa, they came to a mountain region in which nature itself opposed their advance, held by tribes whose courage long kept them at bay; and though the country was reckoned a part of their African empire, they prudently left a good deal of liberty to these fierce warriors as an untamed and untamable race.

The Arab conquest swept over Africa, but left them still in possession of their mountains, and, to a great degree, of their freedom. They became Moslems, yet they took even their religion in a somewhat free and independent way. They would be no man's slave. They clung to their mountain homes, instead of following their new masters into the desert, and retained many of their ancient customs, their women never veiling their faces after the manner of the East. Such were the Berbers, so famous in the history of Northern Africa; and such are their descendants, the Kabyles of to-day.

In the many-colored population of Algiers the stranger recognizes a variety of African races, with others that show traces of an Asiatic origin, most of which he can make out, as to what they are and where they came from; but he is a good deal puzzled by one that is neither white nor black, but of a light-brown or olive complexion—a race that stands apart, with its own language and its separate communities, governed by its own laws and institutions. These are the Kabyles, the children of yonder mountains—a people of fiery and impetuous nature, ardent lovers and bitter haters, hard workers and terrible fighters, as they have shown in a hundred wars, from the days of the Romans to the last insurrection against the French. American readers may be interested to read a little more of this country and people.

My first introduction to them was by Mr. Grellet, the father of our Consul, when he took me over his vineyard of several hundred acres, which is cultivated wholly by Kabyles; a hundred of them were at work at that very moment. They were alert and active fellows, of middle stature, lightly yet strongly built, with frames all nerve and muscle, in which toughness was combined with agility. Their eyes were bright, and, as they recognized a stranger, they looked up in my face with a pleased expression, that was in itself a kindly greeting. Mr. Grellet said they were excellent laborers. It was evident that they were in the best relations with their employer, whom they never passed without a "*Bon jour!*" which was perhaps all the French they knew. I was at once struck with the difference in their physique, or, perhaps I should say, in their carriage, from the Arabs, who are more picturesque in appearance, and carry themselves more proudly; while the Kabyles have more stuff in them for work, and are ready to turn their hands to anything, even if they have to stoop to the lowest drudgery. As it was in the winter season, they were busy in grubbing up the old roots, clearing out worthless stocks, or those which had been touched by any insect pest (not the phylloxera, which has not yet made its appearance here), or preparing shoots for planting elsewhere, as Mr. Grellet had an order for four hundred thousand shoots for Tunis. They take naturally to the labors of the field, in which they are a perfect contrast to the Arabs, who look upon such labor as a degradation, and even hire the Kabyles to do work which they are too lazy to do themselves. The Arab is at home on his steed, scouring the desert, while the Kabyle is never seen on horseback. He is content to go on foot, and is not ashamed of honest labor; he earns his money in the sweat of his brow, and, what is better, he knows how to keep it. They are a thrifty folk, living on little, and saving every hard-earned penny.

"How much do you pay them?" I asked.

"Two francs and a quarter [forty-five cents] a day."

That may seem small pay to American laborers, but it is good wages in Africa. All depends on what it will bring. A French *ouvrier* would eat and drink it all up, for he must have his meat every day, and his bottle of wine; while the Kabyle is content to do without either, and thus saves nearly three-quarters of all he earns. He is a true economist; he has made it a matter of exact calculation, and reduced the art of living to a minimum. One who knows them well said to me: "A Kabyle will live on twelve sous a day, two of which he will spend in tobacco, his only luxury."

"These men," said Mr. Grellet, "live almost wholly on bread. Meat they do not touch unless it be on some special occasion, such as a Moslem feast. Every morning the Kabyle cuts off his portion of bread for the day. Sometimes he will cut out the inside of a loaf, and put it to soak in olive oil, which is here so abundant and so cheap, and this makes a nutritious food; and if, with the two sous for tobacco, he can spare one sou more for a small cup of the black coffee of which he is very fond, he asks heaven for no more. This is his daily portion; but if to-morrow should be a rainy day, so that he could not work, he would not give himself the same allowance, and consume a whole day's provision, for that would be eating his bread before he had earned it, and so encroaching on his little capital. He will cut a day's portion in two, and go on half-rations for two days, so that he can 'start even' on the third!"

American laborers, who are the most wasteful in the world, may think this a petty economy, which shows a miserly spirit. "Why do not these poor fellows do as we do, and enjoy their earnings as they go? What is the use of all this saving and hoarding?" So little do we know of what is stirring in these dusky bosoms.

As we stood looking at the different groups, which were not only very busy, but very happy, Mr. Grellet said to me: "Every one of these men, to the youngest [for some of them were little more than stout boys], has the ambition to earn a few hundred francs, with which he will go back to his native village and buy him a wife!" Indeed! and so the fire of love is burning in these African breasts. It is the old story of Jacob serving seven years for Rachel. Love cannot have its reward without toil. No maiden wastes her affections on an impecunious lover. A man must pay "the old gentleman" for the hand of his daughter. It may not be in money, but in sheep or camels, though the thrifty father likes to see the shining pieces of precious metal. On one occasion, at a hotel in the interior, I paid a bill in napoleons, at seeing which the landlord said that there was but little gold in the country; that whenever a Kabyle got hold of a piece, he hoarded it against the day when he might wish to buy him a wife, trusting that, if the old man would not take a camel, his heart might be softened by sight of the glittering coin. This bit of information caused me to look with new interest into the bright faces before me. I saw that the laborer of the Sahel, in the midst of his toil, was dreaming dreams of a cottage in the mountains, and of the little group that in time would gather round the door.

"And how much does one of these mountain maidens cost?"

"*Cela dépend.* A man may get a common-looking girl for a hundred francs [twenty dollars], but the more handsome—and some of them are very pretty—are much higher. One of my men had saved, in the course of two or three years, six hundred francs, all of which he paid for his bride. He did not begrudge the money, for she was the fairest of her village, and in her he saw the mother of a son who would be the pride of his old age. But just as he was looking for his first-born, to his bitter disappointment the son proved to be a daughter! And when this happened a second time, I believe, if the neighbors had not interfered, he would have killed her!" So the ardor of love may be dampened by circumstances not under control.

"And do you trust these men perfectly?" I asked.

"Yes and No! They are good, faithful fellows, industrious and honest, according to their ideas of honesty. But in the time of the vintage, when the grapes are to be gathered, I have to employ two hundred men, and then I must keep a sharp watch. It will not do to leave anything of value about, for they will take it without a moment's hesitation, thinking that Allah has put it in their way, and that it would be a disregard of his gifts to neglect the opportunity. Everything is thrown upon Allah. He is not only the inspirer of all good deeds, but the scape-goat for all bad ones. I had a Kabyle who was a good laborer, but who had an incurable habit of petty thieving. He would steal without any motive, taking what he could have had for the asking; and when I charged him with it and said, 'Why do you steal what you can have without stealing? You know that I would give you all the grapes you want,' he was not at all abashed, but threw off the responsibility by saying that 'Allah made him steal it!'"

This lying and stealing are such contemptible vices that an Anglo-Saxon cannot understand how they can coexist with anything that is worthy of respect. And yet these very men have many noble traits, and belong to one of the bravest races in the world.

As they are not only brave, but quick to resent an injury, they furnish an inflammable material that may flame out suddenly into insurrection; and what fighters they can be they showed in the insurrection of 1871. Mr. Grellet was at that time in Algeria, and I asked him if he was in danger?

"No," he said, "the insurrection did not come this side the mountains."

"And is there any danger now?"

"I think not. We are too near Algiers, where there is always a large body of French troops; but still you cannot be sure of anything with races that are so excitable. You cannot restrain them from revolt by showing them that the attempt would be hopeless. They recognize the power of France, because they see French soldiers in the streets; but if it were not for this, it would be very difficult to give them an idea of a power that is on the other side of the sea. Even as it is, you cannot convince them that they are not really stronger than their masters, whom they could 'wipe out' if they had a mind to. This confidence in themselves is kept up by religious fanaticism. The Kabyles, though not so fanatical as the Arabs, are still greatly under the influence of their priests, and think that a marabout (the descendant of a Moslem saint) has some mysterious and irresistible power. One day I was talking with a Kabyle, who was old enough to have good sense, and I said to him, 'How is it that you dare to make war against France, that has an army larger than your whole population?' 'No matter for that,' said the fiery old mountaineer; 'what do we care for your armies? If one of our marabouts were to wave a stick at them and pronounce a curse upon them, he could sweep them all into the sea.'" It did not seem to occur to him as somewhat remarkable, that, if one holy man had such power, all of them together, raging and cursing, and stirring up the tribes to put forth their utmost strength, did not produce more impression, but had finally to give in and make their submission to the French! However, it is best not to ask too many questions. There is no reasoning with fanaticism. Putting aside all foolish boasting, no one who has seen the Kabyles, and least of all those who fought against them, will dispute the courage which has been proved on so many fields of battle.

The Alpine character of this region is increased by the snows upon the mountains. These do not remain through the year, for the mountains of Kabylia are not so high as the Alps; but it is now midwinter, and they are mantled in white far down their sides.

Those who have penetrated into the interior of Kabylia give the most picturesque descriptions of its mingled wildness and beauty. As they go farther into it, the mountains rise higher and the valleys sink deeper. In some places it seems as if the mountains had been cleft asunder by some convulsion of nature, and tremendous cliffs stand facing each other, parted by gorges of almost unfathomable depth, down which the torrents roar, while the eagles soar and scream over the abyss.

There, in those wild mountains, is the home of the Kabyles; for homes they have, to which they cling with all the fondness habitual to mountain tribes. In this, again, their life is in contrast to that of the Arabs, who live on the desert, dwelling in tents, wandering hither and thither, now to this oasis and now to that, wherever they can find subsistence for their flocks and herds; and, as soon as this is exhausted, striking their tents, and disappearing below the horizon.

The Kabyles, on the other hand, live in villages, which are generally perched on some high point of the mountains for protection and defence. Look yonder! We can see them distinctly, and very picturesque they are, clinging to the mountain-side. But if we were to interrupt our journey long enough to pay them a visit, we might find them marked by other features than picturesqueness. In Mr. Grellet's excursion through Kabylia, he passed from village to village, and his descriptions were anything but attractive. Climbing to their heights, he found a village, sometimes perched on a cliff looking sheer down into the vale below, or on the ridge of a mountain, with an outlook on either side. As its space was so confined, the houses were packed together in a solid mass. Streets there were none—at least, which deserved the name—many of the villages being divided only by a single lane, so narrow that two could not walk abreast. The houses are of but one story and one room, in which all the family sleep together, lying down at night on the bare ground, which they share with the domestic animals. As there are no windows, the interior is dark, the door being the only opening for light and air to come in, and for the smoke to go out as it rises from a hole in the ground where the inmates cook their food, like Indians in their wigwams. Of course the air is vile, even on the mountain-top, for all the winds of heaven cannot drive out the smells of such a place. How anything in the shape of humanity can live in these hovels is a mystery; but the fact that the Kabyles do live, and not only live, but increase and multiply, is proof of the vitality of the race. Some of these villages have a thousand inhabitants; indeed, I have been told that there were several with five thousand, but this seems hardly possible. And yet, who can count the bees in a hive, or the ants in an ant-hill? The bees in these hives are certainly not drones; they are busy bees, presenting an example of industry that is a marvel among the idle and indolent populations of Africa.

As soon as a young Kabyle has bought a wife, he must have a little patch of ground on the mountain-side. No matter how rough it may be, he will dig round the rocks, pick out the stones, sow a little wheat and barley, plant a few fig-trees and olive-trees, have his sheep and his goats; and then he will sit before his door and smoke his pipe with a proud consciousness of independence.

The Kabyles have a political life of their own, which

is at once patriarchal and democratic. Each village is a little republic, or commune, governed by its own headmen, and a number of these villages are formed into a rude confederation like the early leagues in the Swiss cantons.

With such simplicity of government, and such industry of the people, a romantic traveller might easily imagine to himself an ideal republic—an Arcadia—throned on these mountain-tops, an abode of happiness which the outer world could not invade. But a community that has no fear of violence from the outer world may yet have elements of discord within, that make it to come short of Arcadia. Such elements there are, even in the heart of Kabylia, whose pastoral people have yet to learn some lessons, not only of household cleanliness and comfort, but of neighborly kindness and peace.

As we were crossing the mountains, I was sitting alone in the railway-carriage, looking at the villages in the distance, when an old officer entered, booted and spurred, and bowed to me with true French courtesy, which seemed to invite conversation.

"You have been long in service in Kabylia?"

"Many years."

"And how do you find the country and the people?"

The country was "*sauvage*," but "*magnifique;*" and the people were "*braves gens*," "*bons pour le travail*," but hot-tempered, quick in anger, and, if it came to war, they were "*bêtes féroces!*" The latter was a harsh imputation; and yet it did not grate on my ears as it might have done, if I had not remembered that at Palæstro the Kabyles threw wounded men into the flames of their own dwellings, and even vented their rage and fury on the bodies of the dead! I now learned that this natural fierceness is not always reserved for open war, but that the people are of a combative temperament; so much so, that, if they have no "grand affair" on hand, they will fight among themselves; that the mountains are full of feuds, in which village is set against village, and neighbor against neighbor. In telling me this the old officer only repeated what has been said by other military men and travellers who have had occasion to explore this mountain region, and who go so far as to say that, when their blood is up, the Kabyles will fight not only with their fists, but with their teeth and nails, biting and tearing each other's faces like panthers of their own forests; and, that if nature's weapons are not sufficient to decide the quarrel, they will seize the gun or the yataghan.

But while we do not cover up this fault of quarrelsomeness, as shown in their feuds and vendettas, we can at least take pleasure in recognizing their courage when displayed against the enemies of their country. Like the Swiss, the Kabyles have an intense love of their country. They love it for its very savageness, in which every peak and crag seems to frown defiance at an invader. They are as jealous of its independence as the brave warriors of Montenegro. Those who have fought for generations against the Turk in the passes of the Black Mountains, overlooking the Adriatic, have not shown more valor than the natives of Kabylia. This courage flames out clearest and brightest in the moments of greatest danger. One custom they have which shows that the blood of heroes is in their veins. When tidings of an invasion come to their mountain retreats, the whole land rises up at the sound of war. The young men of the different tribes enter into a solemn "league and convenant," which might be called the league of death, since all who join in it swear to die for their country. So complete is this offering up of their lives, that the prayers for the dead are read over them, so that when they go forth to battle they are already as dead men, and have only to seek the place where they may give up their lives. If, indeed, they annihilate the enemy, they may return *and live;* but if the foe is still in the field, they must seek death until they find it. If one were to flee in the day of battle and return to his tribe, he would be received as the Athenians received the one survivor of Thermopylæ. He would be an outcast in his tribe, doomed to suffer a thousand insults worse than death. But for those who are killed, there is glory here and rest hereafter. Their souls ascend to paradise, while their bodies are buried apart, in a place which is thus rendered forever sacred, and to which pious Moslems will come and pray over the dust of their heroic dead.

One thing more only is needed to complete the picture of Kabyle virtues to be set against the dark background of deeds of violence. They are capable, not only of courage, but of fidelity in the face of great temptations, of which they have given an example, that should be told in their honor, and to which the French owe their empire in Africa. Never was that empire in such danger as in the Franco-German War. As soon as it was evident that it was going against the French, their troops were recalled from Africa to take part in the great struggle at home, till Algeria was left almost without defence.

Then the hour for which the conquered races had long waited had come, and if they could at once have joined their forces and proclaimed a holy war, it is altogether probable that the French would have been driven from Northern Africa. They might have regained Algeria after the German war was over, but only by a repetition of the years of fighting which it cost to conquer it. That the tribes did not take advantage of this, and rise while the French had their hands full on the other side of the Mediterranean, was owing wholly to their fidelity to a solemn pledge.

When the war broke out, a chief of great influence among the tribes, Mokrani, gave his word to the Governor-General of Algeria that there should be no insurrection while the war lasted. That word was faithfully kept. The French arms were followed by disaster after disaster; Napoleon surrendered at Sedan, and Bazaine surrendered at Metz. Then it seemed as if a voice from the Rhine called to the tribes of Kabylia to seize an opportunity which might never come again. But not a man stirred; nor yet when all the defeats and disgraces of the war culminated in the siege and surrender of Paris. The Moslem's faith was plighted; the Moslem's faith was kept! But when all was over, when the last battle had been fought, and the treaty of peace had been signed at Frankfort, then Mokrani was released from his pledge; and then, and not till then, did he declare war. And still he would take no unfair advantage, but gave forty-eight hours' notice. Then the war-cry went through the mountains, and the tribes rushed to the field. They fought desperately, not only destroying towns, but laying siege to fortified places. Even Fort Napoleon, now Fort National, the strongest fortress in Kabylia, had to sustain a siege of over two months before the French troops could come to its relief. But the end was inevitable; for as soon as the French armies were freed from duty at home, they came in large divisions across the Mediterranean. Seeing that all was lost, Mokrani put himself at the head of his troops for the last battle, and dashing to the front, "foremost, fighting, fell."

The war was ended, and the Kabyles were subdued, but with no loss of reputation for courage, and with increase of honor, in that they had kept faith even with unbelievers; and it was fitting that the French should themselves erect a monument to mark the spot where this noble enemy perished. Such fidelity, coupled with valor in war, and industry in peace, with intense love of country, and courage in defending it, are enough to redeem a whole people from the reproach of barbarism.

CHAPTER X

THE GORGE OF CHABET

No man has done so much to bring Northern Africa to the knowledge of the English-reading world as Sir Lambert Playfair, the British Consul-General at Algiers, where he has been for twenty-five years, and has had occasion to make excursions to every part of the country, till he knows it from one end to the other. His Hand-Book on Algeria and Tunis, published by Murray, is altogether the best in existence; while, aside from that, he is himself an encyclopædia of information on a hundred subjects, which could be touched but lightly in such a volume, and on which it is the delight of his friends to listen to him. To his kindness I owe the outline of an excursion which should take me into parts of the country that I had not visited before, and the interest of which I leave the reader to judge.

He advised me, in going east, instead of keeping on direct to Constantine, to turn off to the left and go down to Bougie, from which I should take a carriage and drive over the mountains. This would take me two days, but enable me to see the Gorge of Chabet, "the most wonderful scenery in Northern Africa," of which he had spoken in his guide-book as "hardly to be surpassed in any part of the world;" adding: "There is certainly nothing to equal it within easy range of the basin of the Mediterranean, except, perhaps, in the island of Corsica."

I followed his suggestion, and, on emerging from the

heart of Grand Kabylia, swung round to the north, and bore down toward the sea. The mountains were still in sight, but sinking down into hills, whose slopes were covered with plantations of the olive and the vine, so that it was, like Palestine, "a land of vineyards and olive-yards, and of brooks that run among the hills." This was a delightful close to the day, which began at Algiers, and now ended at Bougie, the seaport of Eastern Kabylia.

When I awoke in the morning, I was in Scotland. As I threw open the window and stepped out on the balcony, I was in the heart of the Highlands. There was Loch Lomond at my feet, with the mountains around it, which, to complete the illusion, were at the moment partly enveloped in a Scotch mist. But the clouds soon cleared away, leaving the mountains in their majesty. Nearly sixty years ago the poet Campbell chanced to light upon this spot, and wrote home in such raptures as these:

"Such is the grandeur of the surrounding mountain scenery that I drop my pen in despair of giving you any conception of it. Scotchman as I am, and much as I love my native land, I felt as if I had never before seen the full glory of mountain scenery. The African Highlands spring up to the sight, not only with a sterner boldness than our own, but they borrow colors from the sun unknown to our climate, and they are mantled in clouds of richer dye. The farthest-off summits appeared in their snow like the turbans of gigantic Moors, whilst the nearest masses glowed in crimson and gold under the light of the morning."

The town of Bougie may be despatched in few words. It has a history dating back to the time of the Romans. There is an old arch that is said to have been reared by them, though it may have been by the Saracens, and an old fort and old walls that have their legends. But I was so absorbed by the mountains and the sea, that I had no eyes for anything else.

The beauty of the morning was but the beginning of a day of varied interest. I was to make my excursion in a new fashion, having done with railroads, as I had done with steamers, and was to be for two days driving over the mountains of Africa.

The only drawback to the enjoyment was that I was alone. It seemed selfish to have a carriage and two horses all to myself; whatever dignity it might give me I would have gladly exchanged for good company. But at least I had a charioteer, who knew a few words of French, and could tell me about the country.

Our course was at first along the bay, where, as we were close to the shore, the waves came rippling up almost to our feet. The country is highly cultivated. There are large plantations occupied by Frenchmen who have crossed the sea to better their fortunes, in which they seem to have been fairly successful. Now and then an avenue planted with trees leads up to a mansion that aspires to take the place of the French chateau. One, I observed, had an under story of massive stone, with portholes, which seemed to indicate that the owner, having in mind the insurrection of 1871, had built a house which, in case of a repetition of that bloody time, might serve as a fortress.

From the bay we came out on the bolder coast of the sea, where the difficulty of construction is increased by the heights to be scaled, and it is sometimes necessary to force a passage by blasting out the side of a cliff. As we rounded the headland of Cape Cavallo, a rock above us bore this significant inscription: "Ponts et Chaussées —1863-64." Only three words and a date! But they tell the whole story: that the department of the French Government which has the special charge of bridges and roads built this road in the years 1863-64. That is the only record of the great power beyond the sea which has given to this portion of Africa a means of communication which the native Arabs or Kabyles, left to themselves, would not have had in a thousand years. To be sure, it may be said that these imperial highways, as well as the systems of railroads, are built by the French to bind together all parts of their African empire. But no matter for that. The roads are here, for the benefit of all races, and will remain to all generations.

To get the full enjoyment of this mountain drive, we had started at seven o'clock, and at eleven stopped to rest our horses. There was no pretentious hotel on the road, but at a place christened "Sidi Rehan" was a farmhouse, that served as a sort of wayside inn and resort of those fond of hunting, as we perceived by the inviting sign, "Au Rendezvous de Chasse." My driver, who was continually going over the road, was familiar with the place, and drove into the yard as one at home. As we entered, the proprietor, in hunting costume, with gun in hand, was starting out for game, but turned politely to bid us welcome. The figure answered to my ideal of a huntsman—not large and unwieldy, but compact and well knit, with an ease and grace of motion that is the natural expression of conscious strength. Besides, there was that which one does not look for in the ordinary hunter—a mild eye, and a voice that was almost feminine in its softness, which made me look up as if I had mistaken the sex of the person I addressed; and I soon communicated to "Sayed" my suspicion that the landlord was a woman, to which he replied that there was no mystery about the matter, and that the proper form of address was not "Monsieur" nor even "Madame," but "Mademoiselle," for that such she was, although of an age when she might be supposed to be married.

Naturally, I was very much interested in the appearance of a woman in this character, but did not suffer my interest to draw me into intrusive curiosity. I simply addressed her as I was told to do, to which she answered without the slightest embarrassment, evidently feeling that her position was as proper as that of any man or woman in the world. Her manner was so simple and natural as to invite conversation, and, as we took our seats under the shade of a large ash tree that stood before her door, I could but remark upon her freedom and independence of life, which led her to speak with such frankness, that she gave me, in the two hours of our stay, quite an outline of her history.

She told me that she was a native of the country, of French parents, but born in Setif, a town on the road to Constantine, so that she was a true "Algérienne." Her father died some years since, leaving a considerable property, and her mother two years since. In the division of the estate there was a disagreement with her brother and sister, that led them to go by themselves; while she, out of what fell to her, bought this place in the country, that she might have an independent existence. It was a bold undertaking, for there were a hundred and fifty *hectares* of ground (three hundred and seventy-five acres) on which there was a large vineyard, the product of which, to judge from a cart that stood in the yard, laden with half a dozen hogsheads, must be considerable. She took me into her garden to show me her orange trees, under which the Kabyles were gathering the ripe fruit. They were not her laborers, but her customers, for she sold them the oranges at thirty-five cents a hundred, and, as soon as the count was made, I saw them pay over the money in silver. All the financial business connected with the estate she attended to herself; for, although it was a large property, what the French would call a *belle fortune*, it required careful management. She told me that when she took it, it was greatly encumbered, and that she had over a hundred thousand francs to pay; but that she had paid more than half already, and in a year or two hoped to pay the rest.

Though she was the sole owner, she did not live alone. She had a manager who took care of the farm, while his wife was her companion. She said they were like a brother and sister to her. This made their little family, while the Kabyles employed on the place, and the people passing on the road, and the hunters coming now and then for a few days' sport in the neighboring forests, kept her from a feeling of loneliness.

So far as this, her story would not have very much novelty. I doubt not there are many cases in our western country where a wife or daughter, left by the death of a husband or father in charge of an estate, has conducted its business affairs with ability and success. Women often show an unexpected capacity in this, as in many other untried spheres of life.

But what has surprised my readers, and perhaps shocked them, has been the putting on of male attire, and with it the assumption of a too masculine style. On these points Mademoiselle was as frank as on others. She admitted that she was not like most women. She said, "I am a character apart. I love the country, and I love my independence. I am fond of an out-door life. I love to mount a spirited horse and ride over the mountains. [She counted it nothing to gallop off thirty kilometres (twenty miles) in a morning.] I love to go into the woods with my gun. [I had observed a couple of double-barrelled fowling-pieces, with a hunter's bag, hanging in the hall.] This is my companion," she said, pointing to a greyhound at her feet.

I asked her what game she found. She said, "There are partridges and other birds in abundance, and wild boars and panthers!" The latter, of course, she never hunted; nor did she at all like the idea of their being near her. A year or two since, while walking in her own grounds, she heard a low growl of one passing in the brush close beside her. Two had been killed this very year. She was glad that they were diminishing, as they were not agreeable neighbors. The offer by the Government of forty francs (eight dollars) a head had brought so many hunters into the field, that they were being gradually exterminated.

Having adopted her manner of life, her costume was a matter of convenience, almost of necessity. With her rough riding in all sorts of weather, the long skirts of a lady's riding habit would be sadly in the way. For the thick woods and mountain heights quite another costume was needed.

It must be confessed that she carried out her own sense of propriety to the full. Her costume was no halfway affair, like that of our fair riders, whose beautiful heads are crowned by a stovepipe hat, while she was in man's attire from top to toe. She wore a soft felt hat upon her head, which had a jaunty look. Her habit was a hunter's jacket of corduroy, with plain steel buttons, and short pantaloons of the same material, ending in a stout pair of riding boots.

And as she dressed like a man, she rode like a man; though, as she took care to tell me, when she went to the city, she took her side-saddle and her riding dress, and rode like others of her sex. But when she was in the free air of the country, she bestrode her horse like a cuirassier, and rode as warriors do when they are riding to battle.

Since writing this, I have been told what leads me to think that perhaps I owe it to my new acquaintance to say that the surprise I felt at her first appearance may have betrayed my own ignorance rather than her singularity; for I have found in these remote parts of the world that the adoption, in special cases, of a masculine attire, is not so uncommon that it need stamp the wearer as braving public opinion by her eccentricity. I am told that an English lady, who is the wife of a French general commanding a division in Algeria, and is fond of accompanying her husband in his hunting expeditions, always prepares herself for roughing it by a costume which enables her to force her way through the tangled brushwood that would tear an ordinary dress to pieces, even though it gives her a little of the look of a soldier. Indeed, the same informant tells me that it has become quite a fashion in certain circles given to cross-country riding and other forms of manly exercise, to which women are becoming more and more addicted, to wear a blouse and belt; and, when the riding is changed for mountain climbing, to exchange the long skirt for one that is not such an impediment to a freedom of motion, which requires the fullest command of both hand and foot.

This more generous interpretation of the singular figure before me is all the more due to her, because, while thus completely attired in a man's costume, there was nothing masculine in her manner, nothing forward or unwomanly. Indeed, I could but think that some of our young women of fashion, who are very "loud" in voice and manner, might take a lesson of quietness and dignity from this huntress of the forest.

Such was the woman whom I met in the heart of Kabylia, whose story enlisted my sympathy, and from whom I parted with a feeling of entire respect. If I tell this story here, it is not that I desire to recommend her mode of life to my countrywomen. And yet it is well to know how men and women live in other parts of the world, that we may give them the confidence which belongs to them. With all her freedom of life, she confessed that she had had a great deal of sorrow. The separation from her brother and sister was a constant grief; and in parting from her, it was with a real sympathy for the loneliness that must at times come to her woman's heart, and a hope that she may hereafter return to society, and find all the happiness that a true woman can deserve.

As we resumed our journey, we found the country rugged and broken, but it was not till the middle of the afternoon that the mountains closed in upon us, as if to bar our further passage. We had been going up, up, up, and now began to go down, down, down, until we entered a defile, where the Alpine chain had been cleft asunder ages ago, leaving only a narrow pass that had been worn still deeper by a mountain torrent. But while this forced a passage for itself, it had left room for nothing else, so that there was not even a footpath by which a man could make his way along the rushing river. There were depths that had never been touched by any human foot. Even the Arab, though sure of foot as the mountain goat, had only climbed over a few accessible points, and crept down into the abyss below, when, as if frightened at his own rashness, he had turned and climbed back again.

To carry a road through such a pass was one of the boldest projects of an age fruitful in great achievements in the way of scaling heights and bridging depths. The engineer had nothing to guide him but the river, but he reasoned that where the waters had forced their way, man could follow; and so he began with pickaxe and drill, and gunpowder and dynamite, to tear away the sides of the mountain. Of course he could not make a straight road: the wonder is, that he could make it at all; which he did only by twisting and turning from side to side, till at last the great barrier was broken through.

And now, following in the path of the conqueror, we sit at ease in a carriage, and roll smoothly over the highway that he has builded, while we look up at the stupendous cliffs reared by an Almighty hand. To describe these so that others shall see what I saw is impossible. Words are tame in the presence of such wonders of nature. Nor is it within the reach of the painter's art. Salvator Rosa might have taken his seat on some projecting crag and sketched a single view, but even he could convey no adequate impression of the mighty whole. I can only say that I have seen nothing grander in the Alps. Indeed, the nearest parallel to it is in our own country, in the Black Cañon of the Gunnison, in the Rocky Mountains.

In this long succession of mountain views (for the Pass is between four and five miles in length) there was that which was not only impressive, but oppressive. If the first sensation was a thrill, the next was a shudder at the prison walls that closed in upon us. There was something awful in the ever deepening shadows which shut out the light of heaven till we felt that we should never more look upon the face of the sun. We had, like Jonah, "gone down to the bottom of the mountains, and the earth with her bars was about us forever." We knew something of that "horror of great darkness" which creeps upon the soul as it enters the valley of the shadow of death. This impression was increased by the stillness and the absence of life. Not a sound broke the silence, save the roar and dash of the waters below. Nor was there a sign of a living thing, save the monkeys that make their home among the rocks. Now and then a bird shot across the darkness, as we could see when the flash of a wing caught a ray of sunlight. Yet all the while we could not resist the fascination of looking upward, though it made the head swim. A mile above us a colossal mass of rock seemed poised in air and toppling to its fall, and we could hardly resist the feeling that it would break away and thunder down the mountain side and bury us forever. So strong was the impression that we were being entombed alive, that it was a relief when, after an hour of this stress and strain, we emerged into the light and sunshine.

In this tender light of the afternoon, we drove out of the Gorge of Chabet, and down the mountain, to the village of Kharata at its foot, where we spent the night.

But here did not end our drive, for as I had made a long detour to compass all that I had seen, it took another day to bring me back to the trunk line of railway that I had left—a day that had its own interest, though in a different way. We were out of the mountains, but still in the hill country, where the constant change of level, going up hill and down, offered an infinite variety of picturesque landscapes. Often, as we climbed a hill, we looked down into a deep valley, where the eye rested on what at first seemed to be a group of haystacks, but what, on looking closer, we found to be the thatched roofs of cottages clustered together—roofs that stoop so low that the eaves almost touch the ground, and it seemed as if a man must not only stoop to enter his house, but crawl in on his hands and feet. But in such humble abodes live father and mother, with little children tottling in and out, and there is room, even, for the pet lamb or kid. Often three or four cottages are placed end to end, so as to form a square, and the open space between them is filled with sheep and the little black goats whose milk serves as a very important contribution to the family subsistence. We could but admire the way in which the Kabyles plant their cottages in the most inaccessible places, wherever they can find a rod of ground to cultivate. With such tenacity do they cling to the dear old Mother Earth, that they may draw life from her life, not "sucking the breasts of kings," but of one greater than kings, the common mother and nourisher of us all.

As the day wore on, the landscape took on new shapes, new forms, new colors. Not only had the mountains sunk down to hills, but the hills sank down lower and lower, till the eye ranged over a broad, undulating country, like the rolling prairies of the West, in which were grazing not only flocks of sheep, but horses and herds of cattle, signs that we had come into a land of plenty, that was at once more fertile and more cultivated, and that yielded a larger increase.

At three o'clock in the afternoon we drove into the town of Setif, of which I had never heard before, but which has a history dating back to the time of the Romans. Now the old is swept away, and all has become new. The town has been rebuilt, and been walled in and fortified by the French. As I did not know a human being, I strolled about alone, simply watching the life that was going on around me. Crossing a square at sunset, I heard a voice, and, looking up, saw the muezzin on the minaret of the mosque, calling the faithful to prayer. The call was quickly answered by a flock of snowy turbans, that, in their rapid motion, swept by me like a flock of doves, hastening to the place where those tall figures would sink on bended knees, and even prostrate themselves, with their faces to the earth, as they offered their evening sacrifice.

CHAPTER XI

GOING DOWN INTO THE DESERT

THE next morning I left too early to hear even the sunrise call to prayer. I had a little sinking of the heart at starting for the desert alone. I knew the lines:

> "Afar in the desert I love to ride
> With the silent Bush-boy alone by my side."

But I had not even a Bush-boy. As we crowded into the omnibus that was to take us to the station, all sat silent and glum. But, as we emerged into the gaslight, I espied a young man who was certainly not French, and not quite English, and, like the Ancient Mariner, I "fixed him with my glittering eye" till I was sure that he was of "mine own country;" we became friends at once, and had a railway carriage all to ourselves, so that we could turn from side to side to take in all the features of Africa, while in the intervals we could talk of our beloved America.

We were bound for the desert, but I cannot say, "Far off its coming shone!" Indeed, it gave no sign of its appearing. For a hundred miles that we bore southward, the country was one of great natural fertility, if not of high cultivation. Only the mountains were bleak and bare, as if they had been blasted and splintered by all the lightnings of heaven. In this work of destruction the waters have joined with the lightnings, as now and

EL KANTARA. THE GATES OF THE DESERT

then great storm-clouds have rolled up from the Mediterranean, and been driven inland, to burst upon the mountains and sweep the soil from their rocky sides, which are thus exposed to the African sun. Here and there the cliffs rise up from the plain like battlements, with long, sharp crests, not broken by a single tree standing up against the sky. But this does not blight the fertility of the plains below, which are just now in all the beauty of spring. There are smiling landscapes that remind one of Brittany and Normandy, all the more that they are dotted here and there with little French villages. But these grow fewer as we get farther south, till there remain only the black tents of the Arabs, which are so low that they seem literally to squat upon the ground, like their occupants. Yet these tents swarm with life. Children are playing about the doors, while the masters are off upon the plain, watching their flocks of sheep and goats, in which I observed, for the first time, our old friend the American hog! But the most striking object in the distance is the shepherd himself, who is a type and a memorial, the representative of a race, as truly as the Indian on our Western plains. It is the same figure that we recognize under an Italian cloak on the Roman Campagna. That figure is one of the oldest in history. Indeed, that solitary Arab, wrapped in his burnous, answers perfectly to the figure of the shepherds that kept the flocks of Jacob three thousand years ago.

While thus observing the tent-life and shepherd-life of these African plains, we are approaching the famous Pass of El Kantara, through which we are to enter the desert. It is by no means so imposing as the Gorge of Chabet, which is over four miles long, while this is but three hundred yards. But it forms a noble gateway to the new aspect of nature that is soon to appear. As I looked up at the cliffs on either hand, it seemed as if the iron gates swung back before the rushing train, which, as it came on with smoke and flame, was no unworthy symbol of the new civilization that is to conquer the world. As we swept through the pass, we looked forward eagerly, expecting to be overwhelmed by the sight that would burst upon us. But Nature does not make her contrasts so sharp and sudden, and softens the impression of the desert by placing at its very entrance a grove of fifteen thousand stately palms! Looking clear to the horizon, the landscape was still fresh and green, even while we were advancing towards a "great and terrible wilderness." Forty miles from El Kantara brings us to Biskra, where the railroad ends, and it was a surprise, indeed, to step from a luxurious railway carriage into a large and well-appointed station, and yet to know that we were actually in the Desert of Sahara! Yes, in the desert, but not quite of it; for Biskra is an oasis, from which the desert is so shut out by the encircling palms that we are on an island of verdure in a sea of desolation.

This remote spot has one supreme attraction in its winter climate, which, because of the distance from the sea, is never troubled by the mists and fogs that often enwrap Algiers and the Riviera. This has made Biskra, since it came under French control, a fashionable winter resort, with all the features of similar resorts on the other side of the Mediterranean. The town is laid out in the French style, with streets well paved, well watered, and well kept, and shops brilliantly lighted; and, as one sees the French soldiers marching through the streets, and hears the bands playing in the public squares, he feels that he is not yet beyond the limits of European civilization.

But he has not far to go to find the other side of the picture. A few minutes' walk will take him into the part of the town known as Old Biskra, where he will encounter the true children of the desert, the old race, and the old barbarism. To see all the native types together, he has but to visit the market-place. We went on the day before the beginning of Ramadan, the Moslem Lent, when for a month all true believers fast from sunrise to sunset. Of course they were eager to lay in a stock of provisions for the long season of penance and privation, and the market was heaped not only with things to delight the eye, but that were good for food. Here were dates and gums and spices, and wheat and barley, as well as leopard skins and ostrich feathers, and all the precious things of Africa.

But the chief attraction of the place was not in the market, but in the people, among whom were men of tribes which have been the terror of the desert. But the present scene was altogether peaceful, while it was full of the animation common at such very miscellaneous gatherings. Here a blind story-teller sat upon the ground, and told his tale in such musical Arabic that even foreigners could perceive that he was reciting poetry. This touched the Arabs' love of poetry and romance, and many left their buying and selling to gather round the poor blind creature, to whom they listened as the men of Bagdad listened to the tales in the Arabian Nights.

In the crowd of country-folk that poured into the town on this market day was an Arab, who went about with a gazelle, a beautiful creature that followed him like a dog. The natives are fond of domestic animals, and make pets of birds and beasts. The house dog is not more one of the family in our country homes than in the tents of the Arabs. Years ago, when travelling in the desert, I found that an Arab village or camp always betrayed itself by the barking of dogs.

But the most notable pet that has been on exhibition here has been a full-grown lion, that was so tame as to be led about the streets. True, he was not just out of the desert, where he had been taken in the toils, brought in as a prisoner, and subdued by the power of man. He was born in captivity at Marseilles, and showed such singular gentleness that he was not only let out of his cage, but followed his keeper about like a huge St. Bernard dog. When he was here in Biskra he was the show and the pet of the whole community. Not only did children run to see him, but their elders also, who came to look at him when he was stretched under a tree, and, eying him at first from a respectful distance, gradually approached till they would jump over him (a privilege for which each one paid a sou), thinking it would give them courage; and the old lion, whether it was that he was so gentle, or that he was too proud to notice such petty creatures, did not resent the familiarity, whereupon even the women grew bold, and, creeping up behind, gave a bound over the monster, thinking it would make them the mothers of those who should be the heroes of their tribe.

Those who come to Biskra for a winter, expecting to find all the gayeties to which they have been accustomed in Paris or Nice, may be disappointed, for it has not yet had such a flood of fashion that it can take its pleasures on a scale quite so extensive. But in its own primitive

AN AFRICAN PET

African way it has attractions that even the lovers of sport need not despise. If its races are not got up with all the splendor of the Grand Prix, yet it is a picturesque sight when the Bedaween dash by as they ride on the desert. Their feats on horseback always excite the wildest enthusiasm of their foreign spectators. But if one who is quite content with the races in the Bois de Boulogne would have a variety in his entertainment, he can have camel races where the swift dromedaries, trained for the purpose, achieve a speed that takes him by surprise; or ostrich races, in which it is hard to tell whether the winged creatures run or fly; or, if he must have something with more of the element of the chase, he may be interested to see the falconers ride into the field, each with a bird mounted on his saddle-bow (and perhaps another on his shoulder) whose eyesight is keener and whose dash is swifter than that of man. Look at that bearded sheik as he tosses his bird into the air. Instantly it detects any small game running on the ground, upon which it darts with almost the swiftness of lightning. This use of birds in hunting reminds those who have been in India of the use which British officers make of animal intelligence when they go out with the cheetah, a species of leopard that is trained to hunting deer. As soon as it is let loose it snuffs the prey, and, crouching in the tall grass, creeps nearer and nearer, not to spring upon it, but to start it into the open, where the hunter can see it and spur his horse in pursuit; all which gives an excitement to the chase that the hunter could not find if he had to take his gun and plunge into the jungle alone.

But for those of us who care not for the race or the chase, Biskra offers a retreat such as one could hardly find, except in the heart of some great forest. A French gentleman with fortune, leisure, and taste—three things that need to be combined for such a purpose—has devoted himself to forming here a botanical garden, chiefly of tropical plants and trees. As the enclosure is a large one, including many acres, and completely filled, one may lose himself in its shades almost as if he were in the "pathless woods." But these are not pathless, for the grounds are laid out with exquisite taste, wide paths and avenues winding here and there, leading up to innumerable points of beauty. The effect of the sudden contrast —for this tropical garden is on the very border of the desert—is at once a surprise and an enchantment. Here one may spend hours, or even days, sauntering under the avenues of palms, or resting in some quiet nook, and forget all that is painful to eye or heart or brain in this poor, dull, weary world. And when it is remembered that all this is open to the public, it becomes a benefaction beyond all price to the poor as well as the rich; and those who are privileged to enjoy it, if they may not compensate him who provides it, may at least express their grateful appreciation of his generosity.

The one excursion that all who come to Biskra must make, is to the tomb of Sidi Okba, the warrior who, in less than sixty years after the death of Mohammed, carried the faith of Islam across Northern Africa, from Egypt to Morocco, for which he has always been held in a reverence next to that for the Prophet himself; and the place where he is buried has been a sort of second Mecca, to which it was a pious act for Moslems to make a pilgrimage, as they have been doing for these twelve hundred years.

It is a two hours' drive from Biskra, half a mile from

which we had to cross the bed of a river that reminded
me of the Wadys in the Desert of Sinai, since, like them,
its channel is for the greater part of the year as dry as
the desert around it, and yet at times is filled from bank
to bank with a foaming, rushing river. But in a few
hours the flood sweeps by, leaving only a bed of stones,
over which it was hard work for the horses to draw our
carriage. But as we climbed the bank on the other side,
we met a truly African sight in the caravans that came
swinging along the dusty road. There is something
grand in the stride of these marchers of the desert.
Some bore heavy burdens on their backs, whose battered
appearance told of a long, long journey. From whence
had they come? Were they laden with ivory from the
Soudan, or had they made a forty days' or a sixty days'
march from Timbuctoo?

When at last we reached the sacred shrine, we could
well believe that the mosque which covers it was the
oldest in Africa, for it has the dust of ages upon it.
The only attractive thing about it is the view from the
minaret, which is made beautiful by contrast, as the eye
looks over the town to the palms beyond, that to some
degree bury it out of sight. Descending to the floor of
the mosque, we enter with slippered feet, and approach
the sacred spot, where a curtain is drawn aside, and,
looking in, we see what appears to be the warrior's
coffin, covered with a pall, and take for granted that he
is inside of it, and are glad of this assurance that he is
dead, stone dead, dead as a door nail! Indeed, I think
it would have been just as well if this man had never
been born, since he was, like Attila, the scourge of God,
who swept across Africa, killing and conquering, till he
was stopped by the ocean, when he spurred his horse

into the waves up to the bridle, and, lifting his sword to heaven, swore that nothing but the barrier by which the Almighty himself had set bounds to his career kept him from carrying the faith to the ends of the earth, and putting to death all who did not submit to its power! Over the tomb of such a man we do not need to shed tears; on the contrary, our sense of justice is satisfied when we read that at the last he who took the sword perished by the sword. Perchance some pangs of remorse smote him at the end, if he dictated the inscription: "This is the tomb of Okba, the son of Nafa. May God have mercy upon him!" But what mercy could he ask, who had none to give? "He shall have judgment without mercy, who hath showed no mercy."

If making this warrior's tomb a place of pilgrimage were intended to strengthen faith in the religion for which he fought and died, it can only have that effect upon those who have not read the history of Northern Africa. For centuries this was a part of the Roman Empire, and shared in the benefits of Roman civilization. Then it became a very important part of the Christian world. Here lived many of the Christian Fathers. Churches rose on the shores of the Mediterranean, and shone like light-houses far out upon the sea. All this was swept away by the Arab conquest, and a night of more than a thousand years settled down upon Africa. History, which has to tell of such destroyers of mankind as Gengis Khan and Tamerlane, has on its bloody roll the name of no one who was a greater curse to the human race than the warrior who lies buried here.

The heaviest doom of all has fallen upon his own people, as witness this very spot; for it would be hard to find, even in Africa, more wretched specimens of humanity than those that crouch and crowd in the shadow of his tomb. The town is a miserable African village, composed of houses of mud dried in the sun, in which the people live in squalid poverty. Men, with hardly clothing to cover their nakedness, sprawl in the streets, leaning their backs against the walls, idle, shiftless, and worthless. And yet these very men, if they would but rouse themselves from this lethargy, and stand up upon their feet, would show figures as straight as Indians, with a proud bearing, as if they were still the lords of the desert. This Arab stock has in it all the elements of power, and it is one of the indictments against Islam that it has enervated and destroyed a manly and a mighty race. The children, too, come into the world as well favored as other children, with eyes as bright as those of the Italian children that furnish subjects for so many artists. Even when they run after the carriage for pennies, you can but smile at the cunning of the little imps, who give you winks and nods to take you on your weak side, till you toss them a few tuppence, in spite of your better judgment.

But it is upon the women that falls the extreme of poverty and all that it brings. However pretty they may be when young, they have to carry burdens that soon break their backs and their spirits, till they fade, and at last wither up into the hags that we saw to-day, sitting by the road and stretching out their hands in utter want and misery. Such is the curse of Islam upon manhood and womanhood and childhood. Sidi Okba has long since passed from the world, but if his spirit lives, he must see the retribution that waits on crime in the wretchedness that gathers round his grave.

We rode home in a thoughtful mood. It is not a

cheerful sight to look on human degradation, and the darkness deepens when the outer world is also in shadow, as if the curse of God had fallen alike on nature and on man. As the afternoon sun shone on the slope of the Aures Mountains, it brought out in fuller relief their ruggedness and barrenness, making the landscape more dreary than before, till the very winds of the desert seemed to moan over the mighty desolation.

To-night I must confess that Africa sits heavy on my soul. It is the Dark Continent indeed. And is this all to which it has come in the thousands of years of its history—to be given up to the most brutal despotism that ever trampled upon human beings, and to know even religion only in its lowest and most cruel forms, in fetichism and witchcraft, in devil worship and human sacrifices? This is a dark picture. But is there not another side to it? Can we not find some rays of light in all this gloom, some twinkling stars in the dark night of Africa?

CARAVAN LEAVING BISKRA

CHAPTER XII

A RAILROAD ACROSS THE SAHARA

I stood on the edge of the desert, as on the shore of the sea. It was the same "gray and melancholy waste," with nought to break the silence and solitude. There is no life there, for the desert drinks it up as the sea drinks up the river. Whatever ventures out upon it is quickly swallowed up and lost. Here is a caravan on the march! With what majestic stride the camels sweep through this avenue of palms, and sail out upon the ocean of the desert. An hour passes, and they have sunk below the horizon, like the swift ships, and are no more seen. Talk not of the all-devouring sea, but of the all-devouring desert, in which lie the bones of innumerable generations, until it has become the sepulchre of the world.

What an expanse it must be to receive these armies of the dead! It spans the continent, beginning on the Atlantic, and stretching to the Red Sea, except where the Nile bursts through it, and makes one strip of verdure that is called Egypt. Nor does the desert limit itself to Africa; but, leaping over the Red Sea, reappears in Arabia Deserta, and again in Persia, and even far away in Beloochistan, at the foot of the Himalayas. This is what is known to geographers as the Desert Belt, which binds like a girdle of fire so large a part of the habitable globe.

But taking only the portion of desert which is in Africa, the Sahara is a continent in itself. It is longer than the

Mediterranean, larger than Russia—larger, indeed, than all Europe, leaving out Norway and Sweden. "It is longer than the earth, and broader than the sea."

In this single fact lies the great barrier to African civilization. The cause of degradation is not moral, but physical. It is not because the people are more debased than other races of men, but because the very configuration of the continent forbids their expansion by a free intercourse with the rest of mankind. This is the burden of Africa, that weighs it down more than a thousand Atlas Mountains.

It is not the mere extent of the Sahara that makes it so formidable, but its position as relative to the whole continent. If it were off somewhere by itself, detached from the rest of Africa, or connected with it only by a narrow isthmus, as are North and South America, it might remain forever a blasted, blighted portion of the earth's surface, miserable itself, but doing no harm to others. But the Sahara has no idea of giving place to anything or anybody, but plants itself right in the forefront of Africa, and takes the lion's share of the continent, shouldering off its neighbors into nooks and corners, or crowding them into the sea. Thus it dislocates all the internal relations of the continent, and does, in the way of separation, what no device or wickedness of man could ever conceive. If the ancient populations of Africa, North and South, had been at war for ages, and finally built a hundred Chinese Walls to keep them apart, they could not be so completely separated as they are by the Desert of Sahara.

Such is the tremendous burden that Africa has to carry. Is there any way to get rid of it? If it could only be taken out of the continent of which it is the unending curse, and sunk in the sea, the waves would roll over it, and it would be remembered no more forever.

But some have thought that, while the Sahara cannot be taken up and cast into the sea, the sea may be brought to it, by letting in the waters of the Atlantic, whereby the desert would be converted into another Mediterranean. The idea has found favor in some minds from an impression that in prehistoric times it was the bed of a sea; indeed, they think to have found traces of sand dunes left where its mighty waters dashed upon the shore. And so they reason, that, where once the waters stood, they might be made to flow again. But a more careful geological inquiry indicates that the sands of the desert are due to other causes still at work, as they have been at work from the beginning of time—the storms that have swept the plains for thousands of years, in which the rocks have been splintered by lightnings, and worn away by rains, till they crumbled into sand that was swept far and wide by the winds of the desert. Equally misleading is the idea that the Sahara is a vast plain of even surface, and below the level of the sea; whereas a large part of it is a vast plateau, broken here and there by lofty mountains. This disposes at once of any glittering project of a canal to connect the Sahara with the Atlantic; for if there were a canal as wide as the Straits of Gibraltar, with the waters rushing into it as fast, water cannot flow up hill, and the vast area of the Sahara is, on an average, fifteen hundred feet above the level of the sea.

Here then is the Great Desert, the one tremendous reality that can never be forgotten in any scheme to solve the problem of Africa. You cannot ignore it, or hide it, or forget it. You cannot bury it out of sight. You cannot drown it, for in spite of you it will come to the surface, insisting on keeping its head above water and above ground, crowding out fertile portions of the earth, while its barrenness renders it unfit for human habitation. There it lies on the face of Africa, a huge black spot, deserted by man, as it seems to be accursed by God. No man passes by it or willingly puts his foot thereon. Even the lonely caravan, that skims it like a bird, leaves no track behind it any more than the bird in the air or the ship on the sea. It passes and is gone, leaving not a trace of life in man, or beast, or bird, or any living thing. So far as we can see, the desert is an utterly worthless portion of the globe.

With such an incubus covering one-third of Africa, there would seem to be little hope of making anything out of it, since the cause which renders its condition so hopeless cannot be removed. We cannot abolish the desert any more than we can abolish the sea. There it is, and there it will remain forever! We can get over the sea in ships, or under it by telegraphs, so that it is no longer a bar to the intercourse of nations. Is there any way of taming the desert, or of subduing it, so that it shall no longer be a barrier to the progress of civilization? This is the most important question to be settled, as bearing upon the future of Africa.

Of course, if it were left to the native inhabitants, all things would continue as they were from the beginning of the creation. Nor has Europe at large any interest in it. But there is one European power that *has* an interest in it. France has large possessions on this side of the Mediterranean. Algeria and Tunis together make a country as large as one of the kingdoms of Europe, which France has the ambition to enlarge still further, so as to have a great African Empire, as England has her Indian Empire. As part of the material for this she has another great dependency in Senegambia, on the western coast, a country covering four hundred thousand square miles. If this could in any way be united to Algeria, if the two could be consolidated, the new empire would at once assume vast proportions. But the desert blocks the way. It splits the proposed empire like a wedge. It cannot be removed, but is there not some way in which it can be converted into a keystone for the mighty arch that is to span the continent from the Mediterranean to the Atlantic? That is the problem which has long exercised the minds of French statesmen, and which they in turn have referred to their engineers, who are among the best in the world; with what result may be briefly indicated.

First of all, they have shown that it is possible to convert portions of the desert into oases by the sinking of artesian wells. A hundred and forty miles south of Biskra is the oasis of Tuggurt, which had long supported thousands of Arabs, with their flocks and herds, but which was nearly destroyed some years since by the wells becoming so choked up as no longer to furnish a supply of water. Vegetation withered, until the wretched people, stripped of what was to them the very water of life, and too ignorant to be able to renew the supply, were in despair, and began to leave the country. Then the French engineers took the matter in hand, and, instead of trying to clear out the old wells, commenced boring into the solid earth, and in five weeks struck water to such good purpose that a river rushed forth that yielded double the quantity furnished by the great well of Grenelle in Paris. To the Arabs it seemed like a miracle, and they began to sing and dance in the wildest manner to express their joy. The miracle was one which can be wrought wherever men are willing to take the labor or bear the expense. Of course, to accomplish a large result in the way of pasturage or agriculture, it would have to be repeated on a tremendous scale.

But for the purpose of uniting the two vast territories of Algeria and Senegambia, the first necessity is that of direct communication, which can only be by a railroad across the Desert of Sahara. Is this within the bounds of possibility?

Nobody's opinion is of any value except that of one who has made a special study of the subject. In Algiers the American Consul took me to see Mr. Broussais, who has taken long journeys into the desert to survey the field of operation. He did not conceal from himself the enormous difficulties of traversing fifteen hundred miles, with the want of water, the want of wood for railroad ties, the want of everything. He looked in the face the possibility of those sand storms which might bury a railroad train, as they have buried a thousand caravans. All this he had taken into consideration, and yet, looking all obstacles and all dangers in the face, he did not hesitate to assure me that, in his judgment, a railroad across the Desert of Sahara was quite within the resources of modern engineering.

As to building a road across a treeless country, where there is neither wood nor water, he would take a lesson from our own experience in the march across the continent, where materials were supplied by the railroad itself, which, as fast as it was laid down, transported the ties and rails to carry it farther. The same system is pursued by the Russians in building the Trans-Caspian Railroad, which they are extending so far to the east.

As to the route to be followed, he took down his maps and showed me the lines that he had traced. Of course he would take advantage of every facility that nature offered in the numerous oases that are scattered over the desert, which he would use as stepping stones, advancing from one to another, as it were from island to island, in the ocean of the desert. As he approached the southern "shore," he would divide his trunk line in two, with one arm reaching southeastward to Lake Tchad, while the other was swung to the southwest till it struck the bend of the Niger above Timbuctoo, down which steamers could descend to Senegambia.

Such is the magnificent scheme which is now seriously entertained by the French Government. Difficult it is to the verge of impossibility. But this is an age of great enterprises, and we can hardly say that anything is impossible. The cost may run up to hundreds or thousands of millions. But it would be undertaken by one of the richest countries in the world, a country that has already thrown away its millions in less hopeful enterprises. The money that has been sunk in the Panama Canal would go far towards carrying out the project in the Sahara. If Russia can build a railroad across Asia, why should not France build one across Africa?

When I heard a man, who was not an enthusiast or a visionary, talk soberly of an enterprise like this, it took hold at once of my imagination. And especially when I found myself travelling over the road—for it is already begun, the road to Biskra being the first stage of it—it seemed as if the vision were already passing into a reality; and feeling at liberty to indulge in some extravagances, I imagined travellers from the north, fifty years hence, or it may be only twenty-five, coming to the very station which I see from my window, and bustling about eagerly, as they hear the conductor shouting his last call, "All on board for Timbuctoo!"

These are the dreams that I dream here in Africa and in the Desert of Sahara. But were the dream already fulfilled, the desert crossed, and the tide of travel in full course, the whole African problem would not be solved. This would be one step towards it. It would pierce Africa at a vital point. It would overcome the greatest difficulty in her geography. It would touch regions otherwise inaccessible. It would take the Soudan in the rear. It would make a direct connection with the western coast, to take the place of the long ocean voyage.

But while the Desert of Sahara is the greatest barrier to its civilization, it is not the only physical disadvantage with which poor Africa has to contend. Another is found in her climate, one of the greatest factors in the life of any country, since on it depends not only the vigor of its warriors, but the strength of a whole people. The line of the equator crosses Africa near its centre, while it passes a hundred miles south of Singapore, the most southern point of Asia. Thus it cuts Africa in two, so that the central portion of the continent lies within the tropics. Was there ever an instance since the world stood, of a great empire that was pivoted on that burning line? Egypt and Carthage were in the extreme north, where they had the bracing air of the Mediterranean to give life to their busy populations. But in the heart of Africa, man is crushed by nature. Nature itself may flourish. Trees will grow where men perish. Mighty forests spring out of the very swamps that sap

IN THE DESERT OF SAHARA

human life. Exposed to enervating heat, it is not strange that Africans sink into idleness. What race could keep its vigor under such conditions? Would those who despise them do better? If the most hardy men of the north, our own New Englanders, or the Highlanders of Scotland, were transplanted to the valley of the Congo, how long would they remain the men that they are? If they were not carried off by fevers; if they became so far acclimated as to live in Africa; they might retain somewhat of their native vigor for one or two generations; but by and by their iron frames would bend, and they would find how grateful it is to take refuge from the noontide heat under the shade of palms. Next to the Sahara, the climate of Africa has done more than all else to decide her fate. Her doom has been written in the heavens, in the fiery sun over her head. This is her misfortune, but certainly not her fault. Did she choose her climate? Did she distribute the land and water of the globe so that her bared and naked breast should lie under the burning sun of the equator?

"But all Africa does *not* lie under the equator. This is true only of Central Africa, and not of the lake regions of the north, nor of the more healthy regions of the south." Yes; but even these more temperate zones are not exempt from a curse, for where they border on the sea, they are shut in by a pestilential coast, which renders them difficult of access to the outside world. The continent is hemmed in on both sides—whichever way it looks, whether it faces the Indian Ocean or the Atlantic—by a jungle of swamps and morasses, one or two hundred miles wide, requiring days or weeks to cross, at the risk of life, before reaching the highlands of the interior. This has been the great obstacle to exploration from the east or the west.

Wherever Europeans approached Africa, they found it barred against them, as if the angel of death stood upon the shore with flaming sword, forbidding them to enter. Missionaries, who could not be restrained in their desire to preach the Gospel on the Dark Continent, have often paid for their devotion with their lives. This has spread such a terror along the coast, that some whose duty called them to it for a few days have thought it prudent not to set foot upon it except at certain hours. It has been made a matter of reproach to the Methodist bishops who were appointed to visit Liberia, that they went on shore only in the daytime, and came on board ship at night. But with all these precautions, Bishop Haven took the fever and died on his return home. The only man that I have ever known who was proof against it is Bishop Taylor; but he has an iron frame, that is like a coat of mail to ward off all attacks. For most persons the climate is deadly; and it is no unmanly fear, but common prudence, to take every precaution against so great a danger. Still more may those who are called to Africa, not by duty but by interest, be excused if they think it wiser to turn their enterprise to other quarters of the globe.

But in what condition does this leave the native population? They have no ships to take them to other countries, save, alas, the Arab *dhows*, laden with slaves, that hide in inlets along the coast, till they can steal out at night, and cross the Red Sea, and land their wretched cargoes. This want of commerce is a privation for any people, even though they were the most intelligent and cultivated, for continual movement to and fro is a part of the life of nations as truly as of the life of the sea. It is like the circulation of blood in the human body. If a man does not stir out of his place, he must be able, at least, to let his thoughts fly, like the birds of the air, which must be kept on the wing if they would not sink to the earth, exhausted and dying. All great nations have been commercial nations, from Greece and Phœnicia to England and America.

But Africa, poor Africa, is excluded from this free life, enclosed, as she is, as by a prison wall. She cannot go to others, and others cannot come to her. Shut in by her swamps and her forests, she is out of the great currents of humanity that flow back and forth like the tides of the sea, and is thus entirely outside of the life of the world.

Is not this total isolation quite enough to account for her barbarism? Can such a people be anything else than ignorant and degraded? If Africa were brought to the bar of nations to answer for herself, might she not say, "All these things were against me"? Her barbarism does not necessarily imply the worthlessness of her people. Let us not exult over her. It would be more worthy of civilized nations to reach out a hand to lift her out of a condition so solitary, in which she has no helper or defender.

In order to come to her relief, the first thing is to break through this "dead line." Already this has been done to some degree. Hunters have plunged into the jungle for the pleasure of the chase and the excitement of adventure. Trading companies here and there have cut a road through the forests, and launched small steamers on the lakes and rivers, movements that have been favored by different governments. Their motives may not have been the most disinterested, but that does not take from the value of the work they have done. It has, at least, been demonstrated that there is no impassable barrier to some mode of transit across the jungle. Whichever power shall bridge this deadly coast line will render an immeasurable service to the civilization of Africa.

In this review of the causes of the degradation of Africa, I have aimed to plead her cause, by showing that it is not her fault; that her barbarism is not due to her own wilfulness or wickedness; that her people are not sinners more than others. Nor has it been that the curse upon Canaan has fallen upon the whole African race, nor that they are by nature less capable of improvement than Asiatics or Europeans; but it has been largely, perhaps chiefly, owing to physical conditions over which she had no control. The recognition of this will lead us to treat Africa with more respect, as well as more sympathy; with an appreciation of her peculiar difficulties, that shall lead to intelligent efforts for her elevation and reinstatement in the eyes of the world.

In material enterprise for the benefit of Africa, the world looks to France as more interested than any other European power. But the whole work of reclaiming the continent from barbarism is not to be thrown upon one country. Other nations have their part also. Within a few years there has been a partition of Africa among the nations of Europe, and all who claim a part in the great inheritance must accept their share of the responsibility. As all these powers claim to be Christian, it may be said that Christendom has taken formal possession of Africa. Is it to be anything more than formal, as when the Pope divided the New World between Portugal and Spain, thereby giving them license to commit the most horrible crimes against humanity? Is this perversion of the name of Christ to be repeated in this century? And by Protestant as well as by Catholic powers? Not by Portugal or Spain, or even by France;

but by Germany, by England, and by America? Could there be a greater shame to Christendom than the persistence of these countries in forcing cargoes of the most fiery and intoxicating spirits upon the natives of the Congo, in spite of the protests of their chiefs? If this policy is to be continued, Africa has as much to fear from foreign powers as to hope—from their jealousy of one another, their rivalships, their greed, and their rapacity. Let them not be in such haste to spoil the Egyptians! Instead of this, Africa ought to be the ward of all the Christian nations of the world. She appeals to them by her very helplessness. She is weak, and they are strong; she is poor, and they are rich; let them show a princely generosity in supplying her wants, both moral and material. If there could be a Holy Alliance of all Christendom to protect Africa from injustice and wrong, and to give her a Christian civilization, then, indeed, we might feel that the day of her redemption is drawing nigh. When the heart of the continent is pierced by a railroad, with lines converging from the eastern and western coasts, she will be compassed round and invaded, not in a hostile way, from every side. Then will it be an easy matter to put an end to the slave trade, and that "open sore of the world," as Livingstone called it, will be stanched forever. Commerce will find its way, not only across the desert, but along the lakes and rivers, and civilization and Christianity will follow in its train. We shall not live to see it. The work can only be begun in this century; its completion will be the great achievement of the next. Men die, but God lives and works out his own great designs; and what we see not now, even by the eye of faith, may yet be accomplished by the greater courage of future generations.

CHAPTER XIII

FROM BISKRA TO CONSTANTINE

In leaving Biskra we rounded Cape Horn. We had reached the most southern point of our journey: we now returned on our course. In coming up out of the desert the scenes were reversed: instead of going from light to dark, we came from dark to light; from barrenness to beauty and fertility. As we left the wilderness behind us, the desolateness brightened into life till, in the afternoon, we were quite restored to civilization. "Just now," said my companion, as we swept over a beautiful tract of country, "we might be in the Mohawk Valley." "Yes," I answered, "and the parallel would be complete if only our American landscapes had for a background these glorious African mountains."

In all these landscapes the mountains form the most imposing feature. They are very grand, and would be very beautiful if they were clothed with forests. The plains suffer from the same destitution, in which they are like our prairies that have been burnt over by the Indians, after which they spring up fresh and green, but with not a tree on all the horizon. Since the French became masters of the country, they have made extensive plantations of trees. I only wish they had introduced some variety, and not confined themselves to the eucalyptus, which has indeed a rapid growth, and is said to serve a sanitary purpose in swampy regions, as its widespreading roots drink up the moisture that might otherwise produce malaria, while the tall trunks supply the country with telegraph poles; but which for ornament, for beauty or for shade, is not to be compared with many of the native trees of Africa and of America. It is not to be named beside the African palm, the English oak, or the American elm. It has not even a second or third rate place among forest trees, for it is ill-favored in every feature. Its whole figure is lank, lean, and dyspeptic; with spindling trunk, spindling branches, and spindling leaves. It is an unsightly product of nature to be transplanted even to Darkest Africa. Its one virtue is its power of drawing water, and for that it might well be planted in swamps, to serve the homely but useful purpose of a long-handled pump, to suck up what cannot be drained off, and thus turn the dank morass into a meadow. If it really affords some protection against malaria, I would that it were planted all along the African coast. And let it be grown for telegraph poles, or bean poles, or even for the fireplace. Wood that is good for nothing else may be good to be burned.

But I do protest against the disposition, in some parts of America, especially in our Western States, to adopt the eucalyptus as an ornament of private grounds, or to plant it along the streets of our new towns and cities. It is not a native of America. It comes from another continent and another hemisphere, even all the way from Australia. I will not say that it is an escaped convict that has taken refuge on our shores; that ought not to be allowed to remain, unless furnished with a ticket-of-leave, by the conditions of which it might be sent back again. It would be more gracious to say that it is among trees what the gypsy is among civilized people, an unkempt creature, with torn and tattered garments and dishevelled hair. It has not a single beautiful feature.

In outline it somewhat resembles the poplar, though it has not its symmetry. What traveller in Lombardy has not been wearied by the thousands of poplars along the roads, each one standing "stiff as a poker"? And yet, when set in double rows to form an avenue, leading up to some venerable chateau, they have a somewhat stately appearance, as they stand in line, like grenadiers, as if to keep guard over the ancestral domain, and protect the pride that still lingers there, from the intrusion of this democratic age. But the poplar does not flourish in America. Our climate is not favorable to aristocracy, even in trees; and the poplar, however high it may lift up its head, soon dies at the top, while its branches grow thin and wither, like a proud old family that has gone to seed. But even in its decay the poplar keeps up appearances by retaining, if not "full dress," the one garment that nature has provided to clothe it withal; while the eucalyptus has been stripped even of its bark, till at last it is literally "naked and not ashamed!"

Yet this wretched ghost of a tree has become almost a national symbol in Algeria, perhaps because it shoots up like a gourd. There are large nurseries for its cultivation. I have seen a car loaded with plants in flowerpots for transplanting. I hope it is only a temporary craze which will have its day in Africa, and a still shorter day in America. It would be to disown that which is our country's pride, if we were to invite this uncouth product of another hemisphere to come in and crowd out our native trees—the majestic elm, the broadspreading oak, the walnut and the chestnut, the beech and the birch, and all the varied growths that are the glory of our forests. Our own children are not to be disinherited in favor of this adventurer.

I write thus warmly as a protest against the silliness and affectation that would run after that which is foreign, when our own trees are a great deal better. Not even in England have I seen more beautiful villages than in the Connecticut valley, a beauty created by the simple forethought of our fathers in planting elms on both sides of the wide, long street, where they have grown for a hundred years, till they lift their lofty crowns into cathedral arches above those who walk reverently beneath the mighty shade.

The people of America should not forget, when they are laying out new towns and cities, that they are planting, as well as building, for those who shall come after them; and that in all that pertains to the beauty of their homes, they should exercise such taste, that what they do shall be a joy for future generations.

But trees and plains are soon forgotten in another sight. The glory of the day came with the setting of the sun, which, as it struck across the plain, touched with its last rays a city that was not merely set on a hill, but that might almost be said to be in the clouds, as it stood up with its shining battlements against the evening sky. Every American traveller who goes to Scotland is enchanted with his first view of Edinburgh Castle as it soars above the city at its foot. But how would the impression be increased if the mighty rock were broad enough to bear up the whole city! Then Edinburgh would be what Constantine is. The impression is increased by its isolation; for it stands apart, as it is cut off from the surrounding heights by a gorge, worn in the rocks by a river in the lapse of ages, till it is completely "islanded," and hangs in air above the waters that still rage around it. One recoils with horror as he stands on the very edge of the beetling crags, and looks over and down into the abyss. The same effect I have seen produced by the same cause in but two other cities: Toledo, in Spain, which is thus encircled by the Tagus; and Jerusalem, which is severed from the high plateau, of which it was once a part, by the brook Kedron, that, flowing for thousands, perhaps millions, of years, has cut a channel in the rocks, so that the Holy City is girdled by the two valleys of Hinnom and Jehoshaphat. It was this standing apart by itself which made Mount Zion "beautiful for situation, the joy of the whole earth." But the grandeur had its limitation, for on neither side was the valley so deep but that one could go down into it, and follow it throughout its whole extent, so that he could literally "walk about Zion and go round about her."

One passage, indeed, there is, in the course of the brook Kedron, which is not so tame, where it changes from the quiet valley to the terrific gorge. But that is far away from Jerusalem, where the brook at times swells into a torrent, and has ploughed its way deeper and deeper into its rocky bed, till, at the very end of the plateau, from which one looks off upon the Dead Sea and the valley of the Jordan, the cliffs are literally cleft in twain to open a passage to the plain below. Here it is that the Convent of Mar Saba hangs on the very edge of the precipice, in a way that makes one who looks down from it shudder lest cliff and convent should topple over together, into the yawning chasm.

All this mingled sublimity and terror are doubled at Constantine, as the features of the scene are repeated on a far grander scale, as the cliffs are higher and the gorges deeper. The first approach gives one a start of apprehension. The bridge by which you enter the town

CONSTANTINE

spans the gorge at such a height that you can hardly look over the parapet without having your head swim, a sensation that returns whenever you approach the walls and try to fix your eye on some object far down in the valley.

To get the full impression of a place that is unique on either side of the Mediterranean, one should take a survey from without as well as from within. That we might not lose anything, we were up betimes in the morning, with a carriage at the door, to make the circuit of the city. Recrossing the bridge, we drove round to the other side of the gorge, and for a mile or more along the cliff, where the French have cut a road in the living rock. I doubt if there is another such drive in the world. One must have a steady head not to be made a little dizzy as he is swung along at full speed. It may be a weakness of the nerves, but I confess that I do not like the edge of precipices (in any sense), and keep as clear of them as possible; so that, when we were whirled round the turns in the road, I had a feeling as if we were being hurled into the air, and instinctively leaned to the other side of the carriage, and even turned my eyes away from a depth into which I hardly dared to look. But this apprehension was soon quieted as we passed over the highest point of the road, and sank rapidly to a lower level, till we came to where the slope of the mountain permitted us to walk, and we clambered down the steep, sending the carriage back to the city, to go round it and meet us as we emerged on the other side.

And now we descend to the bed of the river; not to the bottom of the gorge, which is still far, far down, but to a rocky ledge, along which the river flows to the cascade, where it takes its last leap. This is a midway position and a good point for observation. Here we may stop and look up. It is not easy to measure either height or depth by the eye, but accurate measurement tells us that the cliff behind us towers full five hundred feet into the air.

Advancing up the stream, we stand under an arch of rock that spans the gorge, reaching from cliff to cliff, like the Natural Bridge of Virginia. Of these arches there are no less than four, above which the city is pinnacled in air, throned upon a height, and looking down into a depth, that make its situation the most picturesque in the world.

But this is not all; these cliffs make it also strong for defence, and suggest the important part that it might play in war. It is the greatest natural fortress in the world. Where is there another fortress, or another city, that has walls five hundred feet high, or a moat five hundred feet deep? Comparing it with other places strong by nature, and that have been made stronger by the hands of men, we should say that it was Gibraltar and Quebec and Ehrenbreitstein all in one.

This natural strength of Constantine has been fully appreciated for more than two thousand years. Here in the days of Carthage ruled the brother-in-law of Hannibal. A hundred years before Christ, Cirta, as its name then was, was the stronghold of Jugurtha, but was taken by Marius, who made it his citadel. How all this history comes back to me after fifty years! When I was a boy in Williams College, one of the books that formed part of our course in Latin was Sallust's "History of the Jugurthine War." Little thought I then that I should ever be on the ground on which it was fought. After the city was taken by the Romans, Jugurtha tried to recapture it.

From yonder hills, he looked back at the prize he had lost, and raged around it like a Numidian lion. Possibly he might have regained it if he had not been the victim of treachery; but, betrayed into the hands of his enemies, he was taken to Rome, and, according to tradition, starved to death in the Mamertine prison, under the Capitol, which all travellers are taken to see as the one in which Peter and Paul were confined before their execution by Nero. When Cirta became the capital of a Roman province, Sallust was its governor; and they still point out the place on the hillside where his house stood, and another spot outside of the city where were his gardens, a tradition that is confirmed by the fact that there is still an inscription that bears his name.

But no strength of position has saved Constantine from the vicissitudes of war, for it has been besieged and taken no less than twenty-four times. Only a little more than fifty years ago (in 1837) it was stormed for the last time, by the French. The Arabs fought desperately, and when all was lost, three hundred of them, rather than surrender, attempted to let themselves down by ropes over the precipice five hundred feet high. The greater part of these were dashed in pieces on the rocks below.

It is hard to realize all these tragedies that have made this a place of blood, as we walk about it now, when it is in perfect quiet, and a traveller from England or America feels that he is under the protection of law as much as if he were in France itself.

How long this will continue remains to be seen. Certainly the French are strong enough, and always will be (except in the event of a European war, like that of 1870, which calls home the troops, and leaves the country undefended), to put down insurrection and maintain their authority. But wise statesmen desire something more—to win the confidence of the native population, so that they shall be not only submissive to power, but loyal in heart. But it is not an easy matter to win the attachment of a subjugated people, especially if they be of another race and another religion. The late Prefect of Constantine did but repeat what I had heard from the Governor-General of Algeria. Perhaps he does not see Americans so often, and that may account, in part, for the warmth of his greeting. He seemed pleased with my admiration for the wonderful scenery, and took me to a point of view from his own windows, which commanded a prospect that was almost worth going to Africa to see. "What an empire you have here!" I said. "Yes," he answered, "an empire in extent, but not in population. Beyond those hills you have but to travel a few leagues southward to come to a country where there is not a town nor a village, the only inhabitants being a few Bedaween roving from one oasis to another, to get a little herbage for their camels, till you come to the boundless Sahara."

And as to the government of such an empire, he spoke not like one who is always in terror and in fear of danger, but like a brave soldier, who looks danger sternly in the face. "All is quiet now," he said, "but an insurrection may break out at any time. We cannot guard against it, nor even anticipate its coming, any more than that of an earthquake, of which there were twenty-five, large and small, last year, between Constantine and Algiers. One thing we cannot do: we cannot touch the religion of the people. If we did, there would be an insurrection to-morrow!"

This is not a state of things that is conducive to quiet

slumbers; and yet these are the cares of empire, that weigh on those who assume such grave responsibility. In the issue Americans have no interest, except the interest of universal humanity. But that is enough to make them desire that the experiment which the French are now making to govern Northern Africa may be completely successful, and insure to a country long cursed by war an equally long, and far more beneficent, reign of peace.

CHAPTER XIV

LIGHTS AND SHADOWS OF AFRICAN LIFE

It seems a mockery to call Africa the land of the sun, when it is so full of misery. Yet there is in this no contradiction. Every picture has its two sides, the bright side and the dark side, the sunshine and the shadow, and it is well to look at both.

The negro is born a happy creature, and nature is indulgent to him. He has none of the burdens of civilization. His wants are few and simple; and so he gets more out of life, or of the little that life gives him, than the white man who looks down upon him, but who may well envy the poor creature who is always ready to sing and dance, and will burst into laughter on the slightest provocation. Observing these brighter points in a very humble and lowly existence may enable us to put the good alongside the evil, and strike a balance between them. Human nature is the same in every country and in every clime; men are men, and women are women, and children are children, all over the world.

To begin with the children. Childhood is the most helpless state of being, but with an African child it seems to be not only helpless, but hopeless. Doomed from birth to the lowest condition, to be kicked and cuffed at the pleasure of a brutal master, were it not better for him that he had never been born? And yet, though these little Africans may be uncared for, nothing can repress the joyousness of childhood. The children of Africa have their games and sports as well as the children of America. If our sympathizing countrymen and countrywomen could see these

"Young barbarians all at play,"

they would see that fun and frolic and childish glee are not confined to any country or race, but that children are children under the African palms as truly as on the green turf of England or America.

Sometimes children have to work as well as play. But this is no harder in Algiers than in New York, where we have hundreds of street Arabs, who compose the noble army of newsboys and bootblacks, and ply their trades with an energy that commands our admiration. They may be ragged and dirty, but they are not unhappy.

I shall always have a pleasant memory of my little friends the bootblacks of Algiers. What merry faces they had! What snapping black eyes! They are not to be pitied. Indeed, I sometimes thought they were rather to be envied by the children of the rich, who were riding about in carriages; kept, as it were, under glass, like flowers in hot-houses, and never suffered to stir abroad unless attended by servants, to keep them from contact with common earth and common children. What puny, sickly creatures they became! Well might they sigh for the freedom of the *gamins* of the street, who, though they had little to eat, and that of the coarsest food, made up for it by the vigor of their appetites; and though they had but rags to cover them, suffered little, since the African sun warmed their blood, and sent it tingling through their veins.

Next to the children as objects of pity are the women, who are the drudges in all uncivilized countries, the ones to bear all burdens and take all blows. Are they not, indeed, objects of compassion? Yes and no! They are, indeed, the humblest of all God's creatures; the poorest, the weakest, the least able to bear burdens, and yet who have the most laid upon them. Such an one is now before me. I see her yonder on the hillside, sitting under an old olive tree to shield her from the noontide heat. Was there ever a more miserable object? Her feet are naked; her arms are bare. One coarse garment is all she has to cover her and to hide her wretchedness. Wretchedness? No: for there is something else in the picture. What is it that she holds so closely? It is a babe in its mother's arms. Swaddled in rags, it may be, or swaddled not at all; naked as it was born into the world; yet it lives, it breathes. It is indeed but a tiny creature, an atom of humanity that lies there, like a birdling in its nest. But if it draws life from another, it gives life in return, in the thrill of rapture that it sends back into that dark African bosom. It is the joy of motherhood, that fills her being with a happiness that angels never knew. Has not that mother something to make life worth living, and to cause her to lift her eyes to heaven in unutterable gratitude?

But in Africa there is no distinction of sex in this: that all alike, men and women, are miserably poor. Go through an African village, enter their huts, that are as bare of comfort as Indian wigwams. How can the inmates exist? That is the mystery. A few rods of ground, which they can sow with millet or barley, and one black goat, that is cropping the grass before the door, and gives a few pints of milk a day, are all their means of subsistence.

It is, indeed, pinching poverty when a man has to

tighten the girdle round his loins to lessen the feeling of emptiness within. But apart from the physical suffering, the poor are not worse off in Africa than in civilized countries. The pangs of hunger are as sharp and keen in London or New York as in Morocco. But poverty is a protection against thieves, as the poor have little that is worth stealing. In these despotic countries it serves a still further purpose, as a screen from the oppression of the Government, which is the great robber. In all countries it is held to be a misfortune to be poor. But here, unless a man can place himself under the protection of one of the foreign powers, he may find it to be an equal, or even a greater, misfortune to be rich; for the possession of wealth attracts the attention of the government, which always strikes at the towering heads. Many a man has lost his life because he was discovered, or suspected, to have concealed treasures. To this danger, at least, the poor are not exposed; so that the old Bible saying that "the destruction of the poor is their poverty," is here reversed, since their poverty is their protection. To be sure, this security is not absolute. The Sultan of Morocco may not himself stoop to rob the poor; but as he farms out the country to governors, who pay him a fixed revenue, and get all they can for themselves, they are the spoilers. Armed with such authority, the governor of a tribe is not above taking the last bag of meal out of a poor man's hut, or his one ewe lamb or black goat from before his door; so that even poverty is not a perfect protection, though it is in part, and to that extent

"He that is low need fear no fall."

Taking all these things together, the lot of the poor in Africa, hard as it is, is not utterly hopeless: there is a light in the window of the poorest hut in the forest, the token of peace and contentment within. And if, under that lowly roof, there be mutual love and tenderness, all the tyrants on earth cannot prevent an unseen angel descending like a dove, and hovering over that humble abode.

But there is an *if* in the case, that compels us to qualify our estimate of the happiness within, for there is another element that may disturb that innocent repose. The happiness of a people does not depend on laws and governments so much as on their domestic relations. The life of our life—the very core and centre of our being—is in the home, where love is made perfect, binding souls together in the tenderest of all human relations.

But this perfect bliss cannot be enjoyed where husband and wife come together, only to continue thus at their own caprice. In Moslem countries the marriage relation is not of God's ordinance, so as to make it sacred and inviolable, and of course has no assurance of perpetuity. What true love can there be where the choice of a bride is a matter of purchase, and has to be settled, not with her, but with "the old man," who looks upon his daughter as one of his assets, to be parted with only at a good bargain! This may stimulate the young and the strong to work for a bride, as Jacob served seven years for Rachel. But when it comes to a counting of so many pieces of silver, it is degraded to the level of ordinary business. There may be a fancy to be gratified in getting a rustic beauty, but with this there is very apt to be in the suitor the sordid desire to get the full worth of his money! A bride thus won may be easily thrown aside. The tie so lightly formed is as lightly broken.

In all Moslem countries the Koran is not only the supreme law, but the only law, civil and ecclesiastical. The court is next to the mosque, or a part of the same building. In Algiers you enter one door and see the true believers turning their faces towards Mecca, bowing and prostrating themselves; and when you come out, you have but to descend a few steps to enter a courtroom, where the Cadi, a venerable Arab, with a long beard and snowy turban, sits to administer justice. Among his other duties is that of sitting in cases of divorce, which, it can be truly said, he turns off with neatness and despatch. You enter, and find the men sitting on one side and the women on the other, waiting their turns till he shall hear their cases. First the man tells his story, and then the woman tells hers. But it is not probable that the testimony of either avails much, for it is not often that a divorce thus asked for is refused. The Cadi has all power; he can make twain one, or one twain. No long details weary the court and disgust the audience. No proof of unfaithfulness is required or given. It is simply a matter of choice on the part of the husband, who has but to say to his wife three times, " I divorce you," and he is free. If he wished, and the person were ready, I doubt not the Cadi would marry him to a second wife within five minutes! The whole business would not cost much. It is only ten francs for a divorce; and then, as if to tempt him to a new venture, he can be married at half price, so that he need only add five francs and he can depart in pride, if not in peace, to conduct his new wife to her home.

But what becomes of her who loved him and trusted him, and who is now tossed aside? And what of the children who are made worse than orphans? These are questions which the destroyer of his home does not stop to answer.

A friend, who attended the court one day, told me that, generally, the result seemed to be accepted by both parties as a matter of course, with which they were too familiar to be much overcome. It may even have been arranged beforehand by mutual understanding. Some, no doubt, thought it a happy relief to get rid of a cruel husband or an ill-tempered wife. But to others, especially where there were children, the separation had a terrible meaning. While many looked round the courtroom, seemingly indifferent, one poor woman buried her face in her hands and wept bitterly. This breaking up of homes must be, in many cases, a breaking of hearts; and a broken heart is as heavy a burden to carry on the mountains of Africa as in any unhappy home of England or America.

I have been "stirred up" about this matter by a case that has come under my eye in Constantine. I was here six years ago, and had not forgotten the fortress-crowned rock that was like another Gibraltar, and wished to see it again. So the morning after our arrival we were up early, and roused the landlord, and bade him summon at once a carriage and a guide, "the best he could find," at which he called to his man of all work, "Send for Ali!" "Ali? Ali?" The name sounded familiar. "Is he not the same one who took me about when I was here before, and who told me how he had divorced his wife?" "Yes, the very same." He soon turned up, and recognized me at once. He is a Kabyle, and, like most of the men from the mountains, a stout, strapping fellow. On the former occasion, when he had shown me the town, and we had become a little acquainted, I thought it a mark of friendship to inquire into his personal affairs, and asked him if he was married. "Yes: he had a wife, and had had one before her," upon which I took for granted that he had suffered a domestic bereavement, and thought he might still be mourning his loss, and that a word of sympathy would be as balm to his wounded heart. But I soon found that he was in no need of consolation, for that the "dear departed" was still living, and as buxom as ever; but that he had, for some reason not at all affecting her character, put her away, or, to use the softer phrase, sent her back to her father. Without the slightest embarrassment he told me all about it, and how much he paid the old man for her, seeming rather proud of the fact that she cost him four hundred francs (eighty dollars), which he evidently thought a pretty round sum; and that he had done the handsome thing, and shown his appreciation of her, by giving it. I do not doubt that she was worth the money, for if she, too, was a Kabyle, she was probably a maiden light of form and swift of foot, who could climb the heights and descend into the depths, bounding from rock to rock, "like a roe upon the mountains." Ten years they lived together; a daughter was born to them, and had they remained in their Alpine home, they might so have continued to the end. But when he came to the city, he came in the way of temptation. Perchance he was caught by some pretty face, and began to bethink himself of using his freedom to be off with the old love and on with the new; and so he sent away his wife without a touch of pity or remorse. The agony it might cause to her, the parting not only from him, but from their daughter (whom he kept), was nothing to him. It was all so pitiful to think of the discarded wife, robbed at once of her husband and her child, taking her lonely way back to the mountains!

Finding it impossible to touch his conscience, I pricked him in another point, in which a Kabyle is never insensible. "Is it not rather an expensive business for you [he might have been earning five francs a day] to pay four hundred francs for the first wife, and then send her away, and pay seven hundred francs [for he told me the exact price] for the second?" I took for granted that the first "investment" was a dead loss. But now I was to learn for the first time of the cunning device by which the canny Kabyle, who must make a sharp bargain, even in love, provides against such a contingency; for he informed me, with an air of triumph, that when he returned the first wife to her father, the old man was obliged by custom, if not by law, to pay back the money which he had paid for her, which, of course, was so much towards the purchase of one whose father rated his daughter at a higher price. This is what, I suppose, railroad men would call a *rebate* upon returned goods. So thoroughly is the mercantile spirit introduced into the most sacred of all human relations.

Such was the story of Ali, as he told it to me six years ago, and which came back to me, now that I was again in Africa, in the same city of Constantine, and once more looked him in the face. After all these years it seemed possible that he might have some relentings, and now and then send pitying, if not loving, thoughts towards the wife of his youth and the mother of his child. And so I inquired very gently about their present relations: "Of course she is not the same to you now, but surely, Ali, you cannot forget your former wife. Do you not sometimes long to meet, even if it were only as friends?

To see her face? to hear her voice?" The suggestion seemed to trouble him for a moment, but he shook it off. "*Non! non!*" he said, shrugging his shoulders; "*quand c'est fini, c'est fini!*" Yes, yes: that is the end, and the old love which they knew when they sat together in the twilight, at the door of their little hut, she with the baby on her knee, had slipped from underneath their feet like a mossy stone, and rolled down the mountain side, to be seen no more!

I looked at Ali, half in anger and half in pity, for I would not do him injustice; and I do misgive me lest I have given the impression that he was a brute, when he was not. Dull as he was in moral sense, and wanting in natural affection, he was not worse than those around him. How could he, poor ignorant fellow, be expected to set up a higher standard than that of his people, a standard fixed by law and sanctioned by religion?

But the story was a very sad one, and being that of a Kabyle, it gave me a new impression of that mountain paradise, of which I had dreamed so many dreams. When I was riding through Kabylia, and looking up to the heights on which its villages are perched, I tried to picture them as the happy retreats of quietness and peace. But even Mr. Grellet, in whose vineyard near Algiers I first saw the Kabyles, told me that they had a mixture of qualities in their composition; that while they were hard workers, they were terrible fighters; that their little villages, packed so closely together, were often the scene of deadly feuds. And now I saw one element of discord. When a man can buy a young wife, and a few years after, or even months, can turn her off and buy another in the next house, the two families are not likely to be the best of neighbors; there must spring up jealousies and hatreds, that, with such a combative race, often lead to the shedding of blood.

Nor is this source of trouble insignificant because it is a domestic affair. The noise of strife cannot always be shut up within the walls of a house. What begins at home may spread abroad. Family quarrels have often led to bloody wars. This element of social disturbance is to be taken note of, as we watch the barometer to see what storms are coming. A cloud no bigger than a man's hand may rise and spread till it darkens the whole heaven. And so, as I have undertaken to draw with a free hand, and on a broad canvas, the lights and shadows of African life, I put this breaking up of families at the head of all that is dark and dreary. Africa has many woes, but this is the greatest of them all. It is worse than slavery, for slaves can love each other and be happy. It is the curse of Islam which casts its shadow over every African home; and of all the clouds that darken the land, this is the blackest that hangs over this soft blue African sky.

CHAPTER XV

HOW THE MOSLEMS FAST AND PRAY

"The curse of Islam which casts its shadow over every African home!" So wrote I at the end of a chapter which seemed to justify it all, and it did. But I never condemn a man without afterwards trying to clear him from my own condemnation. I could not be a judge, for I should want to give a decision in favor of both parties. That is my weakness: I never say a hard word of any poor sinner, that I am not the next moment smitten with remorse lest I have borne down upon him too harshly, and look about to find some redeeming feature to relieve a judgment that was too severe.

As with an individual, so with a creed or a religion. Men's philosophies are like themselves, not unmingled good or evil, but a mixture of both; of dark and light, of weakness and strength. Thus in regard to the faith which rules so large a part of the Eastern world. While I take back nothing of my condemnation of that feature of it which permits husbands to cast off their wives for the slightest offence, or no offence at all, yet that is not the whole of the Moslem religion. It has other features borrowed from Judaism and Christianity. Its ancient history is that of the Old Testament. The Prophet revered the patriarchs, Abraham, Isaac, and Jacob, and the lawgiver Moses, as his predecessors; while in the teaching of the practical virtues, Islam is largely infused with elements derived from a still Greater Teacher. Certainly we can find no fault with the Koran so far as it follows the Bible; nor with Mohammed so far as he follows Christ.

Much has been said of the spread of Mohammedanism among the tribes of Northern Africa as a thing to be deplored. If it were to take the place of the Christian religion, Yes; but as against the worst forms of paganism, No. Let it have full swing to drive out the old idolatries, the worship of devils, fetichism and witchcraft, and human sacrifices. If it were only to abolish the "Grand Custom," in which hundreds of human beings are slaughtered every year, it would be a blessing to humanity.

So marked is the resemblance in many features to Christianity, that some modern writers claim that Islam ought to be recognized as, if not a twin sister, at least a half sister; as having the same ancestry, and entitled to be looked upon as kindred with it. A year or two since, a Canon of the Church of England, who certainly bears a distinguished name—that of Isaac Taylor—if he does not inherit all the wisdom that belonged to its original possessor—read a paper before the English Church Congress, in which he boldly demanded that Islam should no longer be regarded as the enemy of our religion, but as its friend and ally. He said: "We ought to begin by recognizing the fact, that Islam is not an anti-Christian faith, but a half-Christian faith—an imperfect Christianity. Islam is a replica of the faith of Abraham and Moses, with Christian elements. Though the teaching of Mahomet falls grievously short of the teaching of St. Paul, there is nothing in it antagonistic to Christianity. The higher Christian virtues—humility, purity of heart, forgiveness of injuries, sacrifice of self—these are not the virtues of Islam. The Christian ideal is unintelligible to savages; but the lower virtues which Islam inculcates, the lower races can be brought to understand — temperance, cleanliness, chastity, justice, fortitude, courage, benevolence, hospitality, veracity, and resignation."

Certainly in one point of morality, temperance, abstinence from intoxicating drinks, the Moslems are at once our examples and our reproach. It is the shame of Christendom, that not only are the gin palaces of London crowded with drunken men and women, but that even in dear old Presbyterian Scotland, in Edinburgh and Glasgow, cities proud of their churches and their universities, there is an amount of beastly drunkenness utterly unknown in Cairo and Constantinople.

Nor is it only in the matter of temperance or of fortitude under suffering, and other heroic virtues, that the Moslems set us an example, but in the performance of their religious duties of fasting and prayer. In proof of this I do not give the testimony of one of themselves— an Arab or a Turk—but of one of another faith, a monk, who, wearing the coarse garment which is the robe of his order, and bound by vows as tightly as by the girdle about his loins, knows by experience what it is to be under the strictest religious discipline. It was during my stay at Biskra that I drove out with a friend to the Convent of the White Fathers, the order organized by the late Cardinal Lavigerie with the special purpose of carrying the gospel into Africa. We had no introduction, but rang the bell at the gate, that was soon opened by a man of tall figure, which might have been that of a soldier, with a grave but kindly face, who received us courteously, and conducted us about the grounds. We soon perceived that he was the head of what I may call, without offence, this semi-religious and semi-military establishment. As the order is designed for hard work, it is composed of picked men, such as would be chosen for a military service of great danger. Even while here in their convent, they are like soldiers in garrison, ready to be ordered at any moment to cross the desert and plunge into the heart of Africa. Such men are not likely to be over-indulgent to the loose practices of those of another religion, and therefore it was with a mixture of surprise at his candor, and admiration of the spirit which it showed, that I listened to what he had to say about the faith which it was the very purpose of his order to combat and overcome. As we were walking through the palm grove in the rear of the convent, he suddenly turned to me and said:

"Do you know that this is the first day of the month of Ramadan?" (The Mohammedan Lent, to which they give, indeed, but thirty days, while Christians keep forty in commemoration of our Lord's fasting in the wilderness.) But he immediately corrected himself by adding that, although it was the day according to the calendar (for the date of the beginning of Ramadan, as of the beginning of Lent, is determined by the changes of the moon), yet inasmuch as this particular day, the 18th of March, happened to be a Saturday, which was the Sabbath of the Jews, it was thought better that the two days should not come together; and therefore the Moslems yielded to their brethren of the more ancient faith, and postponed their "opening" to the next day. But the time of beginning was fixed, according to the reckoning of the Jews, from the hour of sunset, instead of midnight;

for at sunset that Saturday evening I heard the firing of guns from the fort in rapid succession, announcing to the faithful that the holy Fast of Ramadan was begun. And from that time till I left Africa—in Constantine, Bone, and Tunis—every day the evening gun told when the hours of fasting were ended, and the faithful might once more partake of food.

But the first notice I received was from the White Father, and I at once pricked up my ears to learn more about this peculiar form of penance, which, while wholly unknown to the Western world, is observed over a large part of two continents, Asia and Africa. The missionaries at Constantinople had told me how, during that month, they were awakened every morning by the thunders from the ships of war in the Bosphorus.

"Yes, yes: I know! Ramadan is the great Fast of the Moslems. But what does it amount to? I suppose they go down on their knees to do penance for a month as a sort of compensation for the sins that they will commit the rest of the year. You know, good Father, that many Catholics are not very strict in their observance of Friday."

A Frenchman is never thrown off his balance, so as to betray his light opinion of another's want of information, or he might have smiled at my ignorance. He enlightened me gently as to the importance of the event in the Mohammedan year, for with all true believers it has a special sacredness. The keeping of Ramadan is a part of the Moslem law, and is enforced by a powerful public opinion. In a Christian country it is no reproach not to keep Lent. Indeed, some intense Protestants make it a principle not to keep it, as if it were conceding something to what they are pleased to regard as superstition. But with the Arabs and the Turks it is not only required that every man keep Ramadan, but it is a disgrace not to keep it, for which one would become almost an outcast among his people.

And as to the manner of keeping it, it is with a strictness almost unknown in the Christian world in the observance of the fasts prescribed by the Church. During all this month devout believers will neither eat nor drink from the rising to the going down of the sun.

Of course, all may not adhere rigidly to this strict rule of abstinence. Some, no doubt, take refreshment in the secret of their houses; and others on pretence of its being required by their health. There are many ways to evade what one does not wish to observe. Who can tell when a man takes a drink of water? Is every man under watch by his neighbor? The higher classes, especially, have opportunities for hidden indulgence, and in Constantinople I was given to understand that the official class observed Ramadan *with limitations*. The Pashas and Beys and Effendis may not hold themselves subject to the strict rules that govern ordinary men, and they can easily take a sip when no cup-bearer is nigh. Then they have a way of cutting short the hours of penance by sleeping in the day time, and waking *and feasting* at night. If their stomachs are empty when the sun goes down, they can eat to the full till the approach of morning, when they can sleep till noon. Thus, by cutting short their waking hours, they make the day of fasting a very short one.

But this mitigation of suffering is obtained only by the more favored class. The workingmen, the laborers, cannot work at night. They must work by daylight, and hence the privation of food bears most heavily upon them, until there can be no doubt that it often issues in the breaking down of health, if not the sacrifice of life. How they can bear it, is more than I can tell. To aggravate their misery, they sometimes work in the fields to the sound of brooks coming down from the mountain side. In this very garden of the convent, there were sluices crossing each other, to irrigate the grounds, through which the water ran swiftly. It seemed to me as if a man set to work here, under this burning African sun, must be driven to madness, and throw himself upon the ground to take one long, full draught, *and die.*

But there are those who are capable of holding in subjection both hunger and thirst. Mr. Grellet told me, that during the fast of Ramadan, so rigidly was it kept by the Kabyles in his vineyard, that from morning to night, though they worked as hard as ever, they touched absolutely nothing; they ate not a morsel of food, nor suffered a drop of water to pass their lips!

Nor do the poor fellows give themselves much indulgence when the long, hard day is done, but turn quietly to their bread and water. However the richer Moslems may compensate themselves for their enforced abstinence, nothing that can be called riotous living can be imputed to the abstemious, hard-working Kabyles. We must confess that this is an example of self-denial that puts all our Christian fasting to shame.

And how do they measure time? There is a borderland between day and night, the morning and evening twilight. When does the day begin, and when does it end? A true Moslem will not cut short the holy hours, but rather lengthen them. He will not wait for the rising of the sun. If there be those who would have a little more slumber, they are rudely awakened by the sound of cannon. At Biskra the guns were fired between three and four o'clock in the morning, to rouse the sleepers to hasten (like the Israelites going up out of Egypt) to prepare the morning meal, knowing that they could taste nothing more until the going down of the sun.

As with fasting, so with prayer. At Tangier I was often awakened by a far-off, lonely cry that came up from the city below. What could it be? A sentinel pacing the walls and sounding an alarm? Or a watchman crying "All's well"? It was the muezzin on the minaret of the mosque, crying to the half-awakened Moslems, "*Sleep is good; but prayer is better!*"

The habit of devotion thus begun, is kept in constant exercise. Five times a day is the call repeated. And no matter where it comes—in the busy city, in the crowded street—it strikes on the ear like a knell, arrests the current of worldly thought, and turns the soul to God. No presence of strangers abashes the devout believer. What are they, poor worms of the dust, like himself, in the presence of the Almighty? God is everywhere, and His presence makes all places holy: whether it be the market or the bazaar, the house-top or the deck of a ship; for the hours of devotion are observed whether on land or sea. I once crossed the Mediterranean with four hundred pilgrims on their way to Mecca, and very impressive it was to see them all rise from the deck at the appointed times, and, standing in ranks along the side of the ship, turn their faces to the east, and bow themselves and worship. But the desert is more lonely than the sea, for here is no crowded ship's company. The camel-rider may be passing over it quite alone, and with the sense

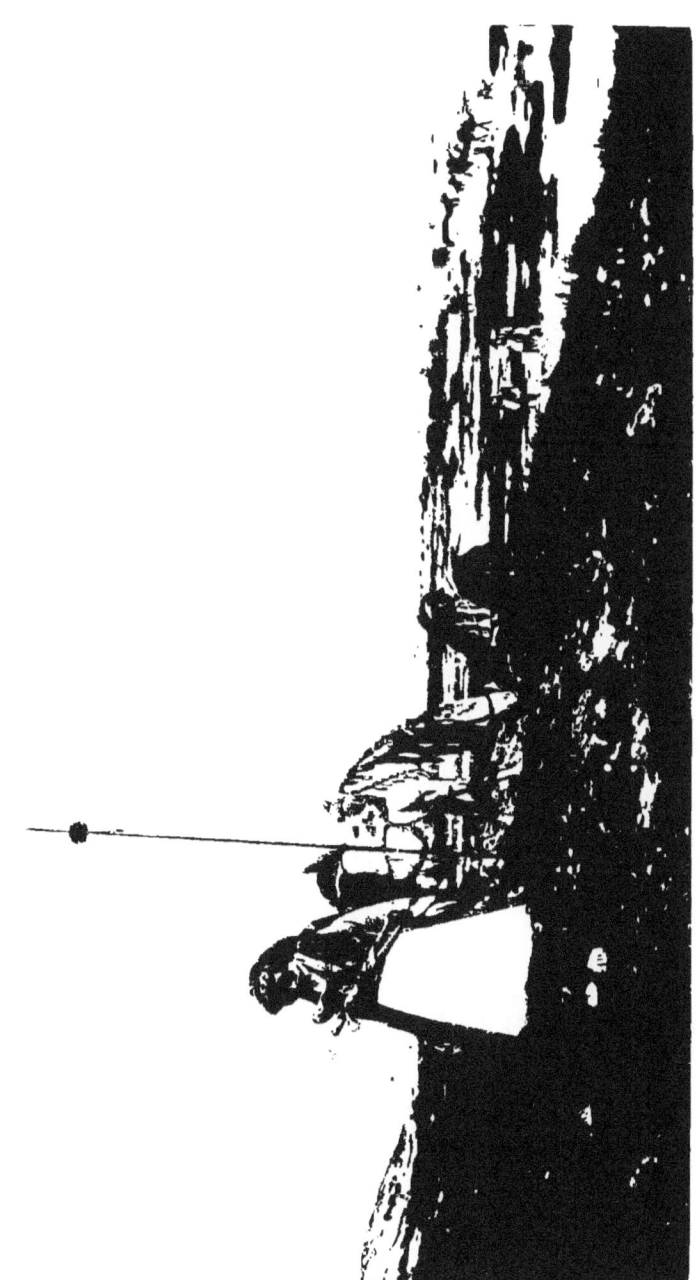

PRAYER IN THE DESERT

of helplessness and need there comes the instinct of prayer. The White Father told me how the poor wanderer knows the hours. He carries no timepiece on his half naked body. But nature teaches the Arab, as it teaches the Indian, simple ways of determining times and distances. He awakes early, for it is the habit of the desert to travel before the sun has risen with a burning heat. There may not be a glimmer of light in the east, and yet there is something which the keen sense of one who lives on the desert interprets as forerunner of the dawn. Drawing a thread before his eyes, he sees only a faint line, with no perception of color. After a few minutes he looks again, and is just able to see whether the thread is white or black. That is enough. Awake! awake! It is the time to pray! He kneels for a few minutes upon the sand, not asking God for protection and guidance so much as pouring out his soul in adoration of the Almighty and the All-Merciful, and then mounts and presses on toward the horizon. But who shall tell him when it is noon? He looks upward and sees the sun over his head: it is on the meridian. Again it is time to pray. Another long stretch, and it seems to be mid-afternoon. He dismounts from his camel, and, turning his back to the sun, *measures his own shadow.* The practised eye gets to be very accurate, but, to make sure, he puts one foot before the other, not a step apart, but touching each other. If ten times the length of his foot be just equal to the length of his shadow, it is once more the hour to pray. Again, at the hour of sunset, he kneels upon the barren floor of the desert as the golden glow flames over it; and his last prayer ascends to heaven as the long, lingering twilight fades in the west, and the stars come forth in the sky.

What means this habit of prayer? Is it ignorant superstition? Or is it a groping after Him who recognizes all true faith as acceptable worship? Condemn Islam as we may, we cannot deny the existence of an intense religious feeling in those who begin and end every day with God.

CHAPTER XVI

LION HUNTING IN NUMIDIA

As we rode down the heights of Constantine, the African Gibraltar, through the wall, and over the bridge that spanned the gorge, we sank down to common earth, the lower level which makes all things common. The spell was broken; but, as we rolled away, we kept looking back, as I had once turned on my horse again and again to take a last look at Jerusalem. We sat motionless till the vision disappeared, when other scenes brought other associations. We were now in the heart of ancient Numidia, the African province which furnished to Rome the lions for the combats in the Coliseum. That race of royal beasts, I took for granted, was long since extinct; as dead as the gladiators whom they fought. But, on coming to Africa, I found that they had an extraordinary tenacity of life, that had outlived many invasions and many wars, outlasting not only the Roman dominion, but the Arab conquest; and, indeed, that lions were the terror of the country till long after the French became masters of Northern Africa. For a time this became the hunting-ground of adventurous Frenchmen, who could not find sufficient excitement in hunting deer in the forest of Fontainebleau.

But now all this romance of the chase seemed to have disappeared before the advance of civilization, and, as we rode over the settled and cultivated country, I as little expected to see a wild beast come out of the forest as to see one spring out of the woods between New York and Philadelphia. And yet the gallant huntress whom I had met in Kabylia, and who surprised me by wearing male attire, had told me that two panthers had been killed near her house but a few weeks before; and that one had passed so near her that she could not only hear his step through the bush, but almost feel his hot breath upon her cheek. But a few days later, I saw, in one of the cities on the coast, a crowd in the street, following a man from the country, who was bending under the burden of a leopard that he had shot in the forest, and was now carrying on his back to the government office to receive the offered reward.

At Duvivier I found an old resident of the place, whom I plied with questions as to his neighbors of the forest. As for panthers (or leopards), they were not so plenty as formerly, but still quite enough for those who were fond of hunting, and altogether too many for those who kept flocks and herds. But the old man evidently thought little of such " varmints" as these. They were small game to one who had heard the voice of something far grander, and could tell how often, on a summer night, as he sat in the moonlight before his cottage, he could hear the lions shaking the mountains with their tremendous roar!

And now we were in the very centre of this country of lions. The principal station on the road to-day was Guelma, which was the headquarters of Jules Gerard, the famous lion-hunter. Some years ago I spent a night at Guelma, and as I sat in the little hotel, before a blazing fire, talking with the people of the country, I was perhaps in the very room where Jules Gerard had sat night after night, before the same fire, with his *camarades*, recounting the adventures of the day. Would that he were here now! What a delight to listen to such adventures from the hero of them all! But since he is not here, perhaps I may give an outline of his story, for though it is years since I read it, it took such hold of my imagination that it is still fresh in my memory; and if we cannot have it before an open fire, it will not be out of place in this railway carriage, as we are passing among the mountains that were the scene of his adventures.

Up to the time of Gerard's coming, the Arabs had been living in constant fear, so helpless were they to contend against the king of beasts. When the lion descended from the mountains into a valley rich in flocks and herds, he was "monarch of all he surveyed." No warrior coming to destroy could excite greater alarm in all the country round. Such was the terror of his presence, that the natives did not dare to be abroad at night, nor to leave their herds exposed, as a missing bullock would serve for the monarch's feast. At nightfall all the flocks were driven into the *douar*, or native village, which was surrounded with a barricade of prickly pear, ten feet high. But even this did not always protect them, for the lion, if he did not find his prey in the plain, followed to the *douar*, and after snuffing round for an entrance, would often clear the barricade at a bound, and striking down a bullock within the enclosure, drink its blood at their very doors.

Terrified beyond measure at the presence of such a destroyer, the natives sought every means to be rid of him. Digging a deep pit, they covered it with brush, and tying a kid near it, tried to lure the lion into the trap. Sometimes a whole village would venture on an attack, and keeping up their courage by numbers and by noise, they advanced against the enemy, who lay in some covert, watchful though motionless, and allowed them to approach, only waiting till they were within reach, when with one bound he sent them flying, often killing dogs and men, and escaping unhurt. If they succeeded in wounding him, and saw that he was crippled, they took courage to come a little nearer, till with their guns and spears they put an end to his career. But the chances were that he would kill a half dozen dogs, and two or three natives, before they brought him to the ground.

In the midst of this universal terror came a Frenchman, who took the field alone, with a single attendant to carry ammunition or an extra gun, but who prudently kept in the rear at the moment of danger.

Though Guelma was Gerard's headquarters, to which he retired like the warrior to his tent after a battle, the scene of his operations was the Valley of Namouna, deep set in an amphitheatre of mountains. He always hunted at night, as that is the time when the lion leaves his mountain retreat and comes down to seek his prey. He chose, if possible, a moonlight night, in which he could see about him, for all he asked was a fair field and no favor. If he could have a full moon, so much the better. At such times the night did not seem long, even though he should watch till the break of day. Alone he sat upon the mountain-side, listening to the winds stirring in the trees, and looking down into the valley where the Arabs were sleeping in their *douar*, or, more probably, listening for the shot which should tell them that they were at last rid of their great enemy. Sometimes he watched all night without success, as the destroyer was seeking his prey elsewhere.

When a lion was the scourge of a whole district, the natives, who were daily witnesses of his depredations, were able to report his nocturnal habits. Gerard inquired of them very carefully the direction of his mountain retreats, and by what path he was accustomed to descend into the valley. Then he placed himself in the lion's path, choosing some spot where he could rest, while waiting, at the foot of a tree, or by some pool in the mountain stream to which the lion came to drink. Here, about midnight, he heard the distant roar which announced that the king of the forest had left his mountain lair and was abroad. He heard it with a thrill of delight, which became more intense as the royal beast came nearer and nearer. At length he heard him coming through the forest, the branches of trees crackling under the leonine footsteps. The hunter almost ceased to breathe as the undergrowth was brushed aside, and the great head came to view in the moonlight, where he could watch every motion. At the same moment the lion saw him, and his heart almost ceased beating as those great eyes glared upon him. Now was the critical moment. An instant's lapse of self-possession and he was lost, for the lion was preparing to spring. The hunter sank upon his right knee, resting upon the left the elbow of the arm that held the fatal weapon. Thus, with his finger on the trigger, he waited an instant, hoping that some sound in the forest might lead the monster to turn his head so as to expose a point between the eye and ear, which was the surest passage to the brain. If, as was sometimes the case, the moon had not risen, or had set, and he was in darkness, he had only to guide his aim those great glaring eyeballs, which shone like lamps in the gloom of the forest. Then he aimed between the eyes. A moment, a flash, a sharp crack of the rifle, and the bullet sank into the lion's brain; and with one spring into the air, he fell at the hunter's feet.

Sometimes the end was not so sudden. Though mortally wounded, the king of beasts still retained strength for a last effort, and the hunter was still in peril, till a second shot had followed in the track of the first.

Then, when the lion was fairly dead, dead beyond waking—for the Arabs were very sceptical on this point, and waited for half an hour to see if he did not utter a deep growl, or strike a last blow with one of his tremendous paws—when the beast was still, the natives who had been lurking on the outskirts of the wood ventured to approach, and at last touching him with their spears, and seeing that he did not resent the familiarity, they fired their guns over the body of the prostrate foe, a fusillade from the mountain which was answered from the valley, in token of the universal joy that the tyrant was dead; that young men and maidens need not tremble as they went forth on moonlight nights, and that their flocks and herds in the valley might rest in peace.

"A pretty tale, 'tis true; but hardly worthy to be included in so grave a chronicle!" But may not even the hunter have "builded better than he knew"? "Nimrod was a mighty hunter before the Lord," and he may have led the way for other messengers of the Lord to penetrate the wilderness. We are not to despise the courage that plunges into the jungle or the forest, or that takes dangers from which others shrink. When Jules Gerard went to Africa to hunt lions, he had no moral purpose whatever, nor a thought of doing good to anybody, but simply of giving himself the intense excitement of hunting the most powerful of wild beasts, the terror of the mountain and the desert, a form of sport which was at once the most daring and dangerous. And yet the result was a great practical benefit by delivering the natives of the country from the fear under which they had been all their lifetime subject to bondage. What all the tribes together had failed to do; what even a regiment of soldiers sent into the mountains might not have accomplished—he did *alone*, with his trusty rifle, his keen eye, his unshaken nerves, and his firm hand. In thus delivering the poor people from their terrible fear, he rendered it possible for them to live quietly in their homes and their villages, the first condition of civilization. In the list of the benefactors of Africa, we must not overlook the hunters, who have often led the way for others to follow. The men who have opened a path into the heart of Africa have commonly preceded or succeeded one another in the order of hunters, traders, explorers, and missionaries; though the order should be sometimes reversed, and the missionary placed first, as in the case of Livingstone, who, in the course of his long journeys in the interior, was a great discoverer as well as an apostle. But we must not despise those sturdy pioneers of civilization who clear a way through the forest by their axes or their guns; remembering that in the description of the happy time when "the wilderness and the solitary place shall be glad, and the desert shall rejoice and blossom as the rose," one feature of its perfect peace and quietness is, that "no lion shall be there, nor shall any ravenous beast go up thereon!"

CHAPTER XVII

THE LAST GREAT MAN OF AFRICA.

WE had been travelling under the shadow of mountains; we were now to come under something greater, the shadow of a mighty name. The glory of a country is its great men, who, by their genius, their elevation of character or force of will, have stamped their impress on an age, and left an example to other generations. Of historic personages Africa has had its full share—mighty kings like Rameses the Great, and the long line of Pharaohs; while over this portion of Northern Africa flames the glory of Carthage and of Hannibal. But Africa can boast of something more than kings and conquerors. The greatest thing that Egypt gave to the ancient world was not her warriors, but her philosophers and teachers. Moses was learned in all the wisdom of the Egyptians, and Plato studied philosophy in Egypt before he taught philosophy in Greece.

In later times something better than philosophy rose upon the shores of Northern Africa, as Christianity spread along the Mediterranean. Here lived many of the successors of the Apostles, the Fathers of the Primitive Church—Tertullian and Origen, Cyril of Alexandria, and Cyprian of Carthage; and, greatest of all, Augustine, whom Archdeacon Farrar crowns with the title of "the last great man of Africa, after whom came the reign of barbarism." Great, not as a warrior like Hannibal, but as a ruler of the opinions of men in all succeeding ages. Augustine has had the singular honor of being venerated alike in Catholic and in Protestant Christendom. In the fierce controversies of the former, his has been the authority to which both sides appealed. Of Jansen, the founder of the sect of Jansenists, it is said: "Ten times he read over every word of Augustine; thirty times he studied all those passages which relate to the Pelagian controversy." All Catholic writers deferred to his great name as if he were inspired. Yet, while canonized by the Church of Rome, he was a leader of the Reformers. It was more than a thousand years after he was in his grave that Luther was born, and yet Augustine was Luther's master and teacher, whose very name he bore (for he was an Augustinian monk); and even after he left the Church of Rome, he still looked up to Augustine as the greatest of the Fathers, regarding him with unbounded reverence, and appealing to him as the highest authority in all matters of Christian faith. The Five Points of Calvinism, including "the horrible decree" (*decretum horribile*), are only a restatement of the harsher features of the Augustinian theology. Traces of the same mighty influence may be found in all Protestant creeds, in the Westminster Confession, and in the Churches of Scotland and America.

He who, after the lapse of more than fourteen hundred years, still rules to such an extent both the Catholic and the Protestant world must surely be accounted one of the great men, not only of the ancient Church, but of all antiquity; and it could not be an extravagance of hero worship that should lead a traveller from beyond the sea to seek out the place where he was born, and to make a pilgrimage to the city in which he spent his active life, and where he died.

Where was he born? A few years ago this question could not have been answered; for though all the biographies (and they have been innumerable) have said that he was born at Sagaste, a town in Numidia, yet so numerous had been the revolutions that swept over Northern Africa, with the frequent change of masters and of languages, that localities were confused, so that the very name of Sagaste was obliterated from geography, and no one could put his finger upon the map and say precisely where it stood. It is only a few years since the uncovering of an ancient monument, with a Latin inscription, led to the discovery of the long-lost site, which was found bearing quite another name, the unmelodious name of Souk Ahras, which, as it was composed of two Arabic words, showed that it had been so called after the Arab conquest.

The place itself is as unattractive as the name. He who goes very far on purpose to see it, will be disappointed, for there is little to see, and the approaches are disenchanting. Even pilgrims to Jerusalem now mournfully confess that the awe-inspiring associations are grievously disturbed when they approach the Holy City by a railroad! And so it disconcerts us to find that Souk Ahras is only a station on the Algerian railway, and that, as the traveller steps out upon the platform, his eye ranges over a mass of railroad shops. And yet a little imagination will enable him to overcome these commonplace realities, and it will be something to "breathe the haunted air;" to look round on the very hills which met the great Augustine when he first opened his eyes on the world, and the fields

> "Where once his careless childhood strayed,
> A stranger yet to pain."

The father of Augustine was a man of some position, though not of high rank. He had but a modest fortune, which he economized to the utmost for the education of his son, who, at a very early age, showed uncommon brightness and intelligence, though nothing that gave promise that he would ever be a saint. Sent to Medaura first, and then to Carthage for his education, he fell into the ways of the gilded youth of his time, the story of which he tells in his "Confessions" with the frankness of Rousseau, though not with such total insensibility to the difference between good and evil. But with all his delinquencies, his natural thirst for knowledge made him an ardent student. It was an age of intellectual activity. Greek philosophy was not confined to the other side of the Mediterranean, but was taught in the schools of Alexandria and of Carthage. Side by side with this was the new religion, which had spread to every part of the Roman Empire, in Europe, Asia, and Africa, where it had to combat the old idolatries. Thrown into such a chaos of opinions, Augustine looked round him with an impartial eye. He was of a speculative turn of mind, and studied all schools and all philosophies. And in the higher sphere of religion he sought for a rational belief with a boldness unrestrained by any fear of consequences to himself in this world or the next. He looked upon a spiritual faith with the same coolness and indifference as upon Greek philosophy; and, comparing one religion with another, his opinion, if frankly given, would probably have been that of the modern sceptic, that all religions were equally true, or, rather, that they were equally false.

While wandering in this maze of speculation, he thought at one time to find a solution of the mystery of the world and of human existence in Manichæism, according to which there was not one God who ruled the universe alone, but two conflicting powers, answering to the Ormuzd and Ahriman of the Persians: a prince of light and a prince of darkness, whose kingdoms bordered each other, and invaded each other, like "the great cloud" in the vision of Ezekiel, with "a fire infolding itself;" the cloud now rolling up the sky till it covered the whole heaven, when the central fire broke through it and drove it away. Every man had two souls: one inclining to good, and the other to evil; and his mission was to subject the latter to the former—a fancy which, if it were taken as an allegory, might be interpreted in accord both with philosophy and religion. For though man has but one soul, there are within the compass of that soul two natures, a higher and a lower, two strong forces that struggle within us, the one combining the reason and the conscience, that are forever at war with the baser passions, with pride and self-will. This was the philosophy of Paul, to which Augustine came when at last he had shaken off the misty vagaries of philosophy and come out into the clear light of Christian truth. But that light he was not to find in Africa. At the age of twenty-nine he left Carthage for Rome, where a wider door was open to genius and ambition. He was a teacher of rhetoric, and a master of that which he taught; so much so, that he soon attracted the attention of the foremost teacher of elocution in Rome, who recommended him to a similar position in Milan.

His removal to that city was the turning point in his life. Milan had then for its bishop one whose name will live forever in the history of the Church as Saint Ambrose, a man who combined in himself the greatest gifts with the noblest character. Not only was he the foremost preacher of his day, but he had in him something more than learning, or eloquence, or even devotion—an extraordinary personality—a love of justice and of truth, with undaunted courage, which gives to him who possesses it a sort of imperial right of command over other men. Ambrose never feared the face of man. When he stood before kings it was not as a suppliant for favor, but as an equal, or even, by right of his spiritual authority, as a superior. He loved righteousness and hated iniquity. He abhorred every form of injustice and wrong; nor did he hesitate to denounce from the pulpit and the altar the ruler, whoever he might be, whose hands were stained with blood. When the Emperor Theodosius, in a fury of passion, had ordered a brutal massacre, and afterwards returned to Milan, he found the doors of the sanctuary shut against him; and, though he had professed Christianity, he was denied the sacraments, and driven from the altar, until he atoned for his crime by the most humiliating confession, and asking pardon of God and men.

A man who thus withstood all the power of a Roman emperor, and who was always the protector of the weak against the strong, was adored by the people. This was a character to excite the admiration of Augustine, who despised inferior men. When the young African first stood amid the crowd that thronged the basilica of Milan, to hear Saint Ambrose, it was as a student and a critic, to learn the secret of his power. But he soon found stealing over him an influence that he could not explain. It was not the sound of the voice; not the music of the words; not even the sublimity of the prayers, nor the chants which still live in the hymns of the ages; but with all this came the conviction that, behind this imposing ritual, this pomp of service, there was a Divine reality. In this man he recognized a character that could be formed only under the influence of religion. When Ambrose spoke to him with the gentleness of one speaking to his own son, Augustine listened and wondered and wept, till at last the change was complete; and on Easter eve, in 387, he was baptized by the hand of one to whom he could look up as truly his father in God.

If that was a moment of supreme interest to Augustine, it was hardly less so to her who had watched over him ever since he was born, and who now stood by his side. Monica was a woman of saintly piety, and her one desire had been that her son might accept the faith that was so precious to her. She trembled for him when he left the shelter of her roof. She followed him to Carthage; she followed him to Rome, and then to Milan; and as she saw him slowly yielding to the wondrous power and fascination of Ambrose, she began to hope; and when, at last, her prayers were answered, her cup was so full that she was ready to die for joy. That joy was prophetic of what was to come.

With the changed feeling that had come into the heart of Augustine, was a changed purpose as to his life; and his first desire was to return to Africa, that, like Paul, he might preach the faith that he once destroyed. Accompanied by his mother, he set out for Ostia, the port of Rome, from which they were to embark for Carthage. As they waited a few days for the ship, they had the full enjoyment of each other's society. Never had their communion been so sweet:

"Ah! little knew they 'twas their last."

Archdeacon Farrar has told the story of their last days together with exquisite tenderness:

"One evening Augustine and his mother were sitting at a window. As they leaned on the window-sill, under the unclouded starlight, looking over the garden and the sea, the sweet and solemn stillness of the hour attuned their thoughts to holy things. They talked together of the kingdom of God. . . . The mother and son raised their whole hearts to heaven, until they seemed to have left all earthly thoughts behind, and enjoyed a foretaste of the hour when the faithful shall enter into the joy of their Lord. Monica said that she had nothing more to bind her to this world. She had desired to linger a little longer, that she might see him a Christian. This desire of her heart God had granted, and now she was ready to depart.

"Augustine enjoyed the glories of nature, and the sea always affected him with peculiar delight and awe. Never could he have gazed over the twilight waves with higher and holier feelings than on this memorable evening. About five days after this happy talk Monica was seized with a fever, and fell into a long swoon. . . . On the ninth day of her illness that faithful and holy soul was set free from the mortal body. She was in the fifty-sixth year of her age. Augustine was thirty-three."

The death of his mother changed the plans of her son. It would be too sad to go alone, and he returned to Rome, and spent a year in study and in writing on those religious subjects which now occupied all his thoughts. Then he began once more to sigh for Africa, and sailed for Carthage, never again to leave the country in which he was born. Returning to the old home at Sagaste, where he had a little estate from his father, he sold it and gave all to the poor, that he might have nothing to turn his thoughts from the service of God. For three years he lived in monastic seclusion with a few friends, devoting his life to study and prayer, and to the writing of what might be a means of instruction to others. His fame spread abroad till the churches turned to him with a desire to draw him from his retreat. But he preferred to be far from the great world. And it was only by the kindly ruse of a friend that he was drawn to Hippo, where the bishop was growing old and feeble; and Augustine was almost literally seized by the people, and compelled to become the bishop's assistant, and, after five years, to be his successor.

It is not often that a man is made a bishop against his will. But so it was with Augustine, as it had been with Ambrose before him. When Ambrose was chosen bishop of Milan he was not even a priest, nor had he been so much as baptized, though he was a catechumen. He was by profession a lawyer, and had shown such ability that he was made governor of two provinces, with his capital at Milan, in which capacity it was his duty to preside at the election of a bishop. There were two parties, and he presided with such a spirit of conciliation, that suddenly the popular feeling turned to him as the man to heal all differences, and he was chosen by acclamation. He tried to escape, but the people would not let him go; and eight days after his baptism he was consecrated Bishop of Milan, and from that moment ruled in the house of God, not only with the dignity of a Roman senator, but with the authority of a Roman pontiff.

Augustine, too, was forced into a place for which he had no ambition. He cared not for power. His tastes were those of a scholar and a monk. He loved the quiet of the country, the walks among the hills, the silence and the solitude, in which he could be alone with God. But he had learned obedience to the call of duty, and when it pointed to a larger field for the exercise of his great gifts, he had only to obey. Thus it was that he became Bishop of Hippo, a city which has lost its ancient name, changing it with its conquerors, till it became Bona, or Bone, to adopt the French spelling of its latest masters. It lies on the coast, sixty miles from the spot where he was born, and two hundred from Carthage. Here came Augustine, in the fortieth year of his age, in the prime of manhood, to enter on the great work of his life; and hither the traveller comes to find some trace or memorial of "the last great man of Africa."

It was evening when we arrived at Bone. The next morning showed us a French town, divided by the Cours Nationale, a broad central avenue, wide enough for open spaces between the drives, with grass and trees, where the people meet to enjoy the summer evenings. It extends to the harbor, in which are lying at all times ships and steamers that trade to all parts of the Mediterranean. At the end of the Cours stands a bronze statue of M. Thiers, in honor of the great statesman who had so much to do with the creation of French Africa.

Of course, my first object was to search out anything associated with Augustine. But the ancient Hippo is gone. Not a trace remains. He died while it was being besieged by the Vandals, and hardly was he in his grave when it was taken and burned to the ground. It rose from its ashes, but fared little better when it fell into the hands of its Arab masters. But now that it belongs to the French, they have a just pride in honoring the memory of one whose name is its own chief distinction.

At the head of the Cours Nationale stands the Cathedral of St. Augustine; and as if one church were not sufficient to keep his name in perpetual honor, another and still grander is now in process of erection on a hill a mile or two distant, in front of which rises a bronze statue of the saint, looking towards the city as if to give it his benediction. In the crypt of the church hangs, among other simple pictures, one of Augustine in his youth, with his beloved Monica, and, underneath, his own touching testimony: "If I do not perish, I owe it to my mother!"

In the rear of the church is a hospital, or, rather, a retreat for the aged and helpless, who have no means of support; and who, instead of being sent to an almshouse, here find a decent home, and are cared for by the Little Sisters of the Poor. Among those devoted to this beautiful charity, I learned that there was one of American birth, and asked if I might see her, to which there was no objection, and she soon appeared in her white cap and Quaker-like dress. She told me that she was from New York, though of Irish descent, where her family were still living. In my innocence I asked her name, at which she was not offended, but answered gently that there were three things which she was not permitted to reveal: her age (which, of course, no one would be so impertinent as to ask), nor her name and family; and, on a moment's reflection, I could well understand that a *religieuse* might not wish to give her address to a stranger, and apologized for the inquiry. What I was more interested and gratified to learn was, that she was not only contented, but happy in her life, with all its monotony, for she never goes outside of these walls. She could go if she wished, and had been several times; but now, apparently, she had no desire to go. Summer and winter, spring and autumn, were alike to her. Day after day it was the same round, watching over the poor, the aged, and the dying. And yet, mystery of mysteries, she was happy, and asked for nothing more. I have observed the same thing elsewhere in institutions of charity and among missionaries, that in doing good to others, they find a fountain of happiness springing up in their own breasts, and filling them with peace. God bless the Little Sisters of the Poor, and all, in any land, or of any creed, who are giving their lives to the relief of human misery!

Though the ancient Hippo has been swept away, the surroundings are the same. Nature does not change. Here are the encircling hills and the broad, open bay, features which are by no means unimportant in the life of a man who, with all his philosophy, had a nature full of poetry, and keenly sensitive to all the aspects of the outer world. The sea had a peculiar fascination for him, and we may be sure that he was not long away from its companionship. There it was, right before him, its waters glistening in the African sun. To this day the most beautiful feature of the environs of Bone is the drive for miles along the bay, winding in and out, now coming down to the water's edge, and now rising to a hilltop on which stands an old fort; and beyond, a bold headland jutting into the Mediterranean. Who can doubt that this was a favorite retreat of Augustine; that he often sauntered along this shore at the eventide, to escape from the littleness of men, or forget the cares of the world, in meditation on things that are unseen and eternal!

For five years Augustine was only an assistant bishop, though his superior leaned upon him more and more, till the title as well as the duties fell upon him, and it was as the Bishop of Hippo that his name became known not only in Africa, but throughout the Christian world. How did he bear himself in his great office?

First of all were his duties as the father of his people. They soon found that he was a father indeed, to whom they could come with the confidence of children. Whoever was in any trouble of mind, in any perplexity of conscience, or in any deep sorrow, was sure to find in the good bishop an attentive listener, a wise counsellor, and a sympathizing friend. He was the father of the orphan, and the widow's stay. Nor did he wait for them to come to him: he went to them. Misery had not to force itself upon him: he sought it out; he went among the poor; he sat by the bedside of the sick; he gave consolation to the dying. Nor did he undertake these duties grudgingly, as if they cut short hours too precious to be given to the poor; but gladly, as a service in which he might follow in the footsteps of Him who went about doing good.

But a man of capacity for things of greatest moment had duties to the Church at large. The beginning of the fifth century was a time of agitation and division. The Church was split into parties, which, if they took their rise in the East, did not end there. All the combatants carried the war into Africa. Against the heretics of the day Augustine was the most powerful advocate of the Catholic faith. But these writings have little interest for us now, that even the names of the heretics live only in history. Who cares to read the long arguments against the Manichæans and Donatists? The controversy with Pelagius has more interest, as the question of foreordination and decrees, as against grace and free will, is still at issue between Calvinists and Methodists.

The mass of these controversial writings is almost incredible, and shows his immense intellectual activity. Perhaps there is too much display of these weapons of war, as it gives the bishop a martial appearance, as if he were a soldier holding a fortress, with guns pointing in every direction; a figure which, however heroic, is not that of the Good Shepherd leading his flock in green pastures and beside the still waters.

In reading the "Confessions," it is impossible not to feel that his theology grew, in part, out of his personal experience. As he had seen the temptations of Carthage and of Rome, he could well believe that the whole world was lying in wickedness. As he had been snatched as a brand from the burning, it was a natural inference that it was by a special election of God that he had been called out of darkness into His marvellous light. We see, also, in that sensitive nature, the reflection of what was passing in the outside world. He lived in one of the most awful periods of human history. The Roman Empire, that had been master of the world for hundreds of years, was breaking to pieces, and, in the general wreck, he may well have thought that the bulk of the race was doomed to destruction, and that there were few that would be saved.

As an interpreter of the Scriptures, Augustine cannot be ranked very high, since he could not read them in the original tongues. He was not a scholar like Origen or Jerome; he knew nothing of Hebrew, and little of Greek, and had to rely, even in his own devotions, on a Latin translation; so that it is not surprising that he fell into errors of interpretation, that are easily exposed by modern scholars.

But a man need not be a great scholar to be a theologian, which requires rather a philosophical habit of mind, in which theology is evolved like any other system of pure speculation.

This habit of mind Augustine possessed in a high degree, and no sooner did he accept the facts of the origin of Christianity than he began to philosophize upon them, and sometimes drew conclusions that are staggering to simple-minded believers; so that, with all our reverence for his authority, we must still reserve our liberty. His inexorable logic may drive us to conclusions from which nature revolts. For my part, I cannot see the difference in the application of logic in the two great religious systems of Northern Africa. The Fatalism of the Mohammedan seems to me only Augustinianism gone to seed; the doctrine of predestination and decrees, carried out to its utmost extreme, so as to include all space and all time, and all that passes in the conscious life of men upon earth—all the thoughts they think as well as the acts they do, all virtues and all crimes, the wickedness of the wicked as well as the goodness of the good, with their inevitable issues in heaven and hell.

Extreme Calvinists (who, in following Calvin, are really following Augustine) should consider, also, how far Augustine carried his orthodoxy; that he shut up the grace of God within very narrow bounds. He was a rigid sacramentarian, believing devoutly in baptismal regeneration, and that outside of the Church there was no salvation! True, he shrank from what it involved, the shutting out from all hope of those who could not know of Christ, and tried to soften their fate by qualifying the "horrible decree" to this extent, that they would receive a milder punishment, what he calls *levissima damnatio!* But even the lightest damnation is damnation still; and his opponents might well protest that it was not easy to reconcile this with natural justice, or with the teachings of our Lord himself, who, in the division of mankind into those on the right and the left of the Eternal Judge, makes no mention of baptism nor of faith, but only of such acts of humanity as feeding the hungry, clothing the naked, and visiting the sick and those in prison.

But for those who could not escape with the "lighter damnation," because they could know and did know of Christ, there was another alternative, from which Augustine did not shrink. He believed in the Church, not only as the depository of Divine truth, but as the inheritor of a temporal power which could be, and should be, used to repress unbelief. Repress is a gentle word; but repression by law means the use of force, of pains and penalties, to compel submission.

And yet Augustine was not "a hard man," who was insensible to the sufferings of others. The intolerance came not from his heart, but from the inexorable logic that works like one of the destructive elements of nature, the storm or the earthquake, breaking down and crushing whatever comes in its way. Having accepted the belief that outside of the Church there was no salvation, it was a natural inference that any means might be used to bring men into the only place of safety. Had not the master of the feast bidden his servants to "go out into the highways and hedges, and *compel* them to come in"? If "the kingdom of heaven suffereth violence, and the violent take it by force," may not violence and force be used also to drive men into the kingdom of heaven? It might even be accounted an act of mercy that their bodies should be burned that their souls might be saved.

And thus the great name of Augustine was used for a thousand years to justify all atrocities and all crimes—the rack and the stake; the Inquisition, and the massacre of St. Bartholomew. When Calvin burned Servetus, he was only carrying out the spirit of his great master. The act of the one followed the teaching of the other. Both show where intolerance and persecution begin; and how good men may be led by wrong principles, carried out unflinchingly, to do, or at least to approve, what, if done in the name of heaven, is in truth the deed of hell.

Yet Augustine was one of the wisest and best of men. But he fell into the mistake to which the greatest minds are exposed in the construction of systems, whether in science, or philosophy, or religion, viz.: that they think to compress the universe within the limitations of a theory, and thus to reduce it to the littleness of the human understanding. God alone can compass the ocean with a span. Any system is of necessity one-sided, as man is always on one side of that which he observes, instead of being in the centre of a vast circumference. A theory made in advance of knowledge is merely a conjecture; but, even as such, it has its use, as an astronomer may project a line into space. But if he takes this imaginary line as his meridian, he may go astray in all his calculations of the heavenly bodies. So Augustine seems to have taken the Church rather than Christ for his meridian line; and if, in consequence, he has failed to construct a system which is for all time, he has but done what others have done, and his failure is for our warning on whom the ends of the world are come. It should teach us extreme modesty in the expression of opinions on subjects that are abstract and obscure; that we should not speak with an air of assurance, setting ourselves up as teachers;

but, rather, as those who are but pupils in the school of the Great Master, even Christ, learning little by little more of his spirit, that we may follow his example. I put in a caveat against the hero-worship of Augustine, by pointing out what seem to us, at this distance of time, the limitations of his range of vision. But every man must be measured by the age in which he lives, and he who is wiser than his generation should not be judged severely if he does not anticipate the advances of those that come after him. The age of liberty of thought and of toleration of differences of opinion had not come, and did not come in a thousand years. But with full allowance for these disadvantages, and for infirmities that are common to men, it must be admitted that Augustine was one of the truly great men, not only of his own time, but of all times; great in genius, great in character, and great in his boundless influence over succeeding generations.

The impression from his life is increased by his death. As we follow him in his latter years, he grows greater and greater to the end. In the midst of his controversies there came a pause on the occurrence of an event which gave a shock to the whole world. In the year 410 Rome fell! More than eleven and a half centuries had passed since Romulus, seven hundred and fifty-three years before Christ, had laid the foundation of the City of the Seven Hills. From that small beginning had grown a power that, in a few centuries, became the master of the world. In the time of the Cæsars the Roman Empire covered all of civilized Europe, a large part of Western Asia, and all Northern Africa. Of this vast dominion, the city of Rome was the seat of power, into which were gathered the spoils of three continents. Yet in one hour was so great riches brought to nought!

The city had been stormed by Alaric, and for three days the barbarian rioted in the spoils of the Capitol and the palace of the Cæsars. It was as if hordes of fierce warriors were suddenly landed on the shores of England, and began their work of destruction by burning London. The wreck of Rome carried terror and dismay to the other side of the Mediterranean; for what had been in Italy might be—and in a few years was—in Africa. Then, if ever, was needed faith in God; and that faith, so terribly shaken by these events, it was the mission of Augustine to restore. Everything in his mind was seen in the light of religion. And now, after the first shock was over, and he had taken in the terrible reality that Rome had been, like Babylon, brought down to the dust, he turned, with the faith of an old prophet, to another kingdom which could not be destroyed. The Eternal City had belied its name, for it was in ruins; but there was another City, whose builder and maker was God!

Thus out of the fall of Rome grew Augustine's "City of God," on which he wrought for many years, and which remains his chief monument, if it be not the greatest work of all Christian antiquity.

The opening chapters are addressed to the pagan world, for it must be remembered that the worship of the gods had not yet disappeared; there were many who still clung to the old idolatries, all the more because of the calamities that had come upon them, which they ascribed to neglect of the ancient religion, as if the gods would be avenged upon those who had ceased to be their worshippers.

Such pretences Augustine swept away with bitter

scorn, showing that the fall of Rome was not owing to the neglect of the temples, but to the people themselves, their vices and their crimes; to the tyrants who had conquered and crushed every nation in turn, leaving everywhere the traces of oppression and cruelty; while the spoils brought home to Rome only served to swell the luxury by which the stern and simple old Romans of the better days of the Republic had become so enervated as to become an easy prey to the barbarian. The state fell because it was rotten within. No offerings to heathen gods, no burning of incense on heathen altars, could save it from this inward decay.

From this picture of inevitable ruin, Augustine turns to a kingdom that shall not be moved; that is symbolized by the City of God. The title is taken from the vision of John in the Apocalypse, in which he sees "the holy city, new Jerusalem, coming down from God out of heaven." That city would stand forever, because it had its foundation in truth. Here the defender of Christianity had the fullest opportunity to set forth its claims as against all the religions of the pagan world. The subject was one that suited his peculiar genius, as in it he could soar into the highest atmosphere of pure speculation, in which he was at home.

It may be an idle fancy, but I could not help thinking, as I rode along the sea-shore with my mind full of Augustine, that in the time of preparation of his great work he must have come here for help in his studies and his meditations. I imagined him climbing some "high and bending head," as Elijah went up to the top of Carmel to look off upon the Mediterranean. It is the hour of the going down of the sun, and his figure is outlined against the western sky. To a mind at once so sensitive and so devout, communion with nature was communion with God. The great and wide sea was the best earthly symbol of the infinitude of the Creator. The waves that came rolling up the beach were the generations of men that were cast up on the shores of time, only to recede and be swallowed up and lost. The dim and distant horizon was the line where the earth touched heaven. Thus things visible were but shadows of the greater things that were invisible; and he who was at once poet, philosopher, and saint returned to his great work with the fires of genius kindled on the altars of religion.

It is said that Augustine wrought upon the City of God for seventeen years; not continuously, or to the neglect of other cares and duties, which were manifold and incessant. He was still a bishop, to whom hundreds of priests looked for their "marching orders;" he was the leader in the councils of the Church, as he had been in all the controversies of the day; added to which there was no statesman of his time, on either side of the Mediterranean, who had so large a correspondence on public affairs with men in high stations—statesmen and princes, kings and emperors—who heard of his wisdom as of a second Solomon, and were eager to receive instruction from his lips. But with these innumerable diversions, one purpose shone like a star above him, to build the City of God. No matter how slow was his progress: he was willing to toil on, year after year, to complete a work that was to be for all generations.

Answering to its title, this immortal work was a piece of divine architecture, builded and framed together with the pious care given to that which is most sacred. It was a temple which could not be reared in air, but must be settled upon everlasting foundations. Here Augustine found a place for his mastery of all ancient learning, of the philosophy of the Greeks and the wisdom of the Egyptians. Testing these by his vigorous understanding, he found that the greater part had to be thrown away. But he found, also, that which was solid and strong, just and true, and he was not above accepting truth from any source. These fragments of Grecian marble or Egyptian granite were used by him as the early Christians used the arches and columns of ancient temples for their churches and cathedrals. Even if broken and shapeless, they might be hewn into foundation stones for the walls of the city, which were to be completed and crowned by the sublime truths of the Christian faith, all together growing into a holy temple in the Lord. Thus constructed by a patient toil, not unlike that of the returned captives in rebuilding the temple at Jerusalem, this City of God is not unworthy to be compared with that which John saw in the Revelation, whereof it is written : " The city lieth foursquare. And the foundations were garnished with all manner of precious stones." So was this City, adorned with all that could give it light and color, brightness and beauty. Nor would it be thought by many too much to carry the parallel still farther, and to say of that which was reared by human hands, that " it had a wall great and high ; " and that " the wall had twelve foundations, and that in them were the names of the twelve apostles of the Lamb." By such patient devotion, carried through so many long and laborious years, Augustine builded his City of God, from the foundation to the topstone, leaving it to be the wonder of all the ages.

The end of his work found the saint near the end of life. In his seventy-sixth year he could not be spared long to the Church. But little could it have been thought by those who held him in reverence all over the Christian world, that his last days were to be darkened by overwhelming sorrows and to end in gloom.

Ever since the fall of Rome the world had been in agitation and in fear. The Vandals had overrun Gaul and Spain, and in the year 429 Genseric crossed the Straits of Gibraltar, at the head of fifty thousand men, and began to lay waste ancient Mauritania. Moving eastward along the Mediterranean, it was but a few months before his ships were in the harbor of Hippo. As it was now certain that the city would be subjected to the horrors of a siege, the loving priests and people came to their bishop, to implore him to escape while it was possible, and take refuge in a place of safety. For this he had every excuse. He was not a soldier, and could not mount the walls. He was well stricken in years, and could not be expected to endure the coming hardships and privations. But touched as he was by their devotion, he would not yield to their entreaties. When did his people need him if not now? Others might go: he would remain. He would share the sufferings and relieve the terror of the affrighted population. If he should not be spared long to inspire them by his example, he could at least show them how to die.

And so the siege began, and month by month came closer and pressed harder, till the hearts of the bravest began to fail them for fear. But in the time of the greatest adversity, they had but to enter the presence of Augustine to be calmed by his serenity. His faith was never shaken. As he looked out from the city walls at night, he saw the camp-fires of the encircling host; but above the camp-fires were the stars; above earth was heaven; and there was One who could make even the wrath of man to praise him, and by whom, in his own time, that wrath would be restrained.

But the strength of the strong man was broken, and he did not live to see the end. It was at the close of that fatal summer of the year 430, on the twenty-eighth of August—just twenty years from the fall of Rome— that "the last great man of Africa" ceased to breathe.

Could we have looked into that death chamber, we should have seen the perfect contrast of that within from that without. Without was war: within was peace. The siege was still in progress; the barbarians were thundering at the gates; but little was it to him who was passing away from all strifes and storms. It may have been that some beloved priest knelt by the side of the dying, and whispered in his ear the last benediction of the Church to the departing soul: "Go forth, O Christian soul, from this world, in the name of the Almighty God who created thee; in the name of Jesus Christ who redeemed thee! May thy dwelling be this day in peace!" Thus upborne by blessings and by prayers, the great spirit lingered not, but rose above the sound of war and all the sorrows of this troubled world, to the City of God, not made with hands, eternal in the heavens.

CHAPTER XVIII

GOOD-BY TO ALGERIA

AFRICA is a country of magnificent distances. Although I had already travelled, since I landed at Oran, five hundred miles along the coast (a distance as great as that across the Mediterranean from Algiers to Marseilles), I was not yet out of Algeria. In leaving Bone we turned our backs on the sea. The last object in sight was the new cathedral in honor of Saint Augustine, its white walls glistening in the morning sun. At Duvivier, near Guelma, we struck the trunk line of Algerian railways, and, turning to the east, soon found ourselves among the mountains. The scene was familiar, and yet different, for I had been over the same route six years ago; but then it was in midwinter, and the tops of the mountains were white with snow. It was now near the end of March, and the last snow-bank had melted away, leaving only the murmur of trickling streams to make music in our ears. The vegetation had the soft and tender green which is the peculiar beauty of the springtime, while over all was the deep blue of the African sky.

The mountains do not lie in one long chain that can be crossed in a single ascent, but are very irregular in formation, being tossed up on every side, like the waves of the sea. Of course it is not an easy matter to carry a railway across such a broken country. But the greater the difficulty, the greater the engineering skill. In ascending the steep grades the tunnels are frequent, and sometimes it seems as if our fiery charger were playing hide and seek as he plunges into a long, dark cavern, where for a few minutes he twists about like an uneasy ghost, till he has made a complete turn in the bowels of the mountains; and when he shows his head again at some higher point, he is racing madly in the opposite direction. It gave me a feeling of bewilderment, and yet of exhilaration, to be thus swung round and round in the very heart of these African mountains.

At last we reached the highest summit, and began to descend. The coming down was as grand as the going up, as at every descent we were brought nearer to the green valleys and the soft warm face of dear old mother earth.

In these few hours we had not only changed our landscape, but changed our country; for in this passage of the mountains we had left Algeria behind, and come down to the border of what has received the name of Tunisia from its capital, Tunis, as Algeria takes its name from its capital, Algiers.

And now for a come-down from all this greatness! As if man could not be left to behold and enjoy the beauty of nature undisturbed, civilization (!) must thrust in its device to vex the souls of nature's worshippers; and what do we find here in the wilderness but a custom-house (!), which, in this case, has a special ridiculousness from the fact that this is not a border line between two countries, but between two provinces of one country, Tunisia being in reality, if not in form, as truly French as Algeria. As well might New Jersey set up a custom-house at Jersey City for all who cross the North River! However, it is not a great matter. It detains us but half an hour, while we are tumbled out, bag and baggage; and the officials, grave and solemn in aspect, as if they were doing their duty to their country, go through the farce of looking into our trunks. But as they observed French courtesy, we were not ruffled in mind, any more than despoiled of our goods, when we took our seats in the railway carriage and resumed our journey.

It was now the middle of the afternoon, and the sun was behind us, so that every object was distinctly in view. Before us stretched a plain, wide and well-watered (for a river runs through it), which reaches all the way to Tunis, a distance of a hundred miles. No more mountains on the horizon, but only a low chain of hills, just enough to frame in the picture. The broad expanse is thinly peopled, only a few scattered farmhouses breaking the outline, with here and there an Arab shepherd in his white burnous, watching his flocks. But the scene is one of unbroken peace. As the afternoon sun strikes across the plain, it is reflected from many a pleasant object—the thatched cottage, with the cattle round the haystack, chewing the cud; while in the distance one hears "the watch-dog's honest bark." All this gives an almost American aspect to the scene, as if it were somewhere in the newer parts of our own country. And yet this great plain, now so peaceful and still, has been, like the Plain of Esdraelon, a battle-field for the marching and contending of hostile armies. Over it passed the elephants of Hamilcar in that stupendous march which led over mountains and seas—across Northern Africa, across the Mediterranean—which his son Hannibal was afterwards to carry across the Pyrenees and the Alps, till the Carthaginians were at the gates of Rome.

It was ten o'clock at night when we reached Tunis. As we rolled into a well-lighted station, and were driven through the well-lighted streets, I could but think how civilization takes away the poetry and picturesqueness of barbarism. Here am I, after a thousand miles of travel in Africa; and yet I have not been once on the back of a camel, even though I have been on the desert, but have been carried over the mountains as smoothly as I could be over the Alleghanies or the Sierra Nevada. And when I step out of the railway carriage, it is not to find shelter in an Eastern *caravanserai*, to herd with the beasts of the stall, but to take lodgings in a French hotel, as if on the boulevards of Paris! Truly civilization makes all things common!

Ah, yes! Civilization is a great leveller, even in the distribution of the good things of life; it makes it at once more comfortable and more commonplace, till existence becomes one long monotony. There is a little of the wild nature of the savage in us all, and we sometimes sigh, "Oh for a touch of barbarism to relieve the dulness of common life! How much more picturesque it would be!" The Arab on his steed, flying over the desert, spear in hand, is a more dashing figure than the farmer jogging along on his old farm horse. And the desert itself, when the setting sun floods even the barren sands with a golden splendor, is very captivating to the eye and to the imagination. But when it comes to the daily round of common life; to the questions, "What shall we eat, and what shall we drink, and wherewithal shall we be clothed," and to a choice between the house and the tent as a place to dwell in: I must confess that, after a long day's journey, it is good to wash away the dust of travel in a bath, the first touch of which subdues my raptures over the poetry of a state of barbarism; and when I sink into a soft bed, and lay my head on a clean white pillow, and am blissfully conscious of sinking into a state of profound repose, my last murmur is, Blessed be civilization!

CHAPTER XIX

TUNIS—ARAB AND FRENCH

THE next morning, as I threw open the shutters and looked out of the window, I saw that I was again in a French city, as I had been at Bone, divided like that by a broad, open space, a sort of esplanade, with driveways on either side, which there goes by the name of the Cours Nationale, and here of the Avenue de la Marine.

Tunis is not so favored by nature in its position as Algiers. It has not the same magnificent foreground of the sea, nor the same background of the hills. It lies on a level plain, with no features which strike you as you approach it, and give it the dignity of a great capital. And yet it is larger than Algiers, having two hundred thousand inhabitants, while Algiers has but one hundred and fifty thousand. It is in population the third city in Africa, being surpassed only by Cairo and Alexandria.

Although Tunis is one of the oldest cities in Northern Africa (having had an existence long before the time of the Romans or the Carthaginians, even before the founding of Utica "the ancient"), our first glimpse was only a bit of Paris transported across the sea. But the old African city is not far away, and it is full of treasures not to be found in any European capital. Come with me, and I will show you something that will open your eyes. We have only to pass through an arch at the end of the avenue to be transported in a moment from the Occident to the Orient, as we enter the bazaars, which extend over a vast space that is covered in like a tent, and protected from rain and sun either by arches of stone, or by mattings hung from roof to roof, across the narrow streets, as in the bazaars of Cairo, which fill the whole, not with "a dim, religious light," but with soft, cool shadows, as if one were in a grove, a "boundless contiguity of shade." It is a musty old place, and yet one of the most fascinating in the world from the multitudinous life that goes on within it. Here are thousands of people crowded together, who are not abroad for pleasure, but engaged in all the industries and occupations of a city. The streets, or, rather, the passages (for they are hardly wide enough to be called streets), are so narrow that friends are almost forced to walk side by side, or even arm in arm, while even strangers are sometimes brought into a personal contact that is too close to be agreeable. This calls for the utmost good nature, as all have to make way for one another, and if they are wise will do so, not only with common civility, but with courtesy. The proudest Englishman cannot be crowded into such a miscellaneous company without, for the moment at least, laying aside a little of his distant and haughty air; if not, it may be squeezed out of him in a way that will cause at once a loss of temper and of dignity.

But even the most fastidious stranger cannot but catch somewhat of the spirit of this busy, bustling crowd, composed of men of all colors and races, and of all occupations, too; for this is not merely a place of barter, for buying and selling, but of manufacturing also, since the things that are sold are in large part made on the premises. Here "Alexander the coppersmith" plies his trade, and here are skilful workmen in gold and silver. In one stall

STREET IN TUNIS

you may see the silk reeled off the cocoons; in another it is dyed with the delicate colors whose production (if it be not, as is claimed of the Tyrian purple, a lost art) seems to be one of the mysteries of the East; and next the precious threads are woven with the old hand-looms which have been used since the days of Solomon.

Then come the rugs and the carpets, made from the choicest fleeces, and dyed with the richest colors; and he must have more than Roman virtue who can resist such a temptation. And as if they would appeal to every sense, so as to intoxicate with every sensuous delight, there is a bazaar devoted wholly to perfumery, where one may regale himself with the otto of roses, and all the sweet odors of Araby the blest.

But perhaps Young America, if ambitious of military trappings, may prefer to be the owner of an Arab spear, or of one of those long matchlocks that every sheik carries at his saddle-bow. How would you like a Damascus blade? If you are an expert in antique workmanship, you may pick out a Turkish cimeter two hundred years old, that has been stained with blood in the days when the Barbary pirates were lords of the Mediterranean, enriching themselves with the spoils of Europe, and sparing their prisoners that they might have the proud satisfaction of being served by Christian slaves!

But if you are of a more peaceable turn of mind, you may be content with a high-peaked Turkish saddle, covered with red morocco; or you may have it mounted with cloth of gold, so that, "when next you ride abroad" in Central Park, you may be the admiration of all beholders.

To be sure, if you wish to buy something of value, you had better exercise a little of your American discretion, for there is sometimes a perceptible difference between the price first asked and the final purchase. When I was in Constantinople, a rich young American was making the tour of the bazaars, where his eye was dazzled by a suit of armor which he would bring across the sea, and hang up in the ancestral hall. But his ardor was a little cooled by learning that the price was thirteen hundred dollars! However, he did not lose his temper or his patience; but, by the buyer's art of "standing off and on" for a reasonable time, carried off the prize for three hundred!

This was an extreme case, but it illustrates the need of caution. And still there is such a thing as carrying caution too far, by which we lose what we very much desire to have. When we were in Tangier, my friend Richard Harding Davis saw in a shop a gun that took his fancy. The price was twelve dollars; he offered eight. The next day a fellow-traveller brought it into the hotel, having paid fourteen, and said he would not take fifty for it, at which Davis was much chagrined that he had lost his opportunity.

In all this it is a good rule "not to be wise overmuch." Do not be in such a mood of watchfulness as to spoil the enjoyment of your first experience, but take the bazaar for just what it is—a curious exhibition of Oriental life, which furnishes, perhaps, the best opportunity to study the Oriental character. I go to it, not to make a sharp bargain, but to observe the men of the East as they differ from the men of the West. There is something that soothes you like sweet music in the soft Oriental manners, in which you may be conscious that you are being beguiled by a subtle flattery, and yet you rather enjoy it. I sometimes get a lesson that makes me feel that I am but an untamed barbarian compared with these men of long beards, white turbans, and flowing robes. When I was in Cairo, I went to the bazaar in company with a missionary who spoke Arabic, so that he could give me the flavor of Oriental expressions. Seeing a rug of very rich colors, I asked him to inquire the price. In the softest voice the Arab replied, "What is that between thee and me?" Could anything be more delicately expressed? It put us at once into new relations—not that of buyer and seller, but of friend to friend—relations of confidence, so that the matter of price was one of indifference. I was unto him as one of his own tribe, of whom he would scorn to take advantage. Not to be outdone in courtesy, I could not let the generous owner throw this treasure at my feet, and when my friend drew from him the consideration for which he would part with it, as it seemed rather large, I ventured modestly, and with downcast eyes, to offer something less, which he did not resent as a desire to depreciate what he valued so highly (he was too well bred for that); but he replied, "more in pity than in anger," that to accept it " would be a shame to his beard," at which I felt that I had almost offered an affront to his dignity.

Of course this will be looked upon as a fine bit of comedy; but it is that kind of comedy which is all the time being enacted before us in real life, and in which the Orientals are greater adepts than we, and play their parts with more exquisite grace. All their little arts, such as the offering of a seat under the tent, or on the divan, and the bringing of coffee and pipes, are a part of the play, which cannot fail to amuse one whose eye is not too critical. In this mood I enjoy nothing more than a morning in the bazaars, where, as I never make large purchases, I do not need to be constantly on my guard. Nor would I be; for a habit of suspicion is more troublesome to him who has it than to anybody else. If I cannot quite say with Hudibras:

> "No doubt the pleasure is as great
> Of being cheated as to cheat,"

yet I had rather be cheated moderately than to be always on the watch. Let them play their parts: I will play mine.

Fascinated by this glittering panorama I wandered on and on for hours, whithersoever my guide would lead me; for indeed I could not have found my way alone, since the narrow passages wind round and round, as in a labyrinth, so that, if left to myself, I should have been as helplessly lost as if I had been in the Catacombs of Rome. But the visit is worth a journey to Tunis, if it had nothing else to show; and I may add, for the satisfaction of those who are not able to extend their travels to the East, that they will find here an Oriental bazaar, if not as large, yet as varied and complete, as if they made the journey to Cairo or Damascus or Constantinople.

When I came out of this bewildering maze, and returned to the Grand Hotel, I felt that I had made a voyage to Africa and back again, for I was once more in Europe. Everything was French—the houses and the people, the shops and the *cafés*. And when I saw French soldiers in the streets, and red-legged zouaves and Turcos pacing up and down before the palace of the Resident and the public offices, it seemed as if the French were here to stay; and an American, with true national impertinence, could hardly help asking how they came here. By what whirligig of fortune are the French now masters of this country? How came they over the border, and what business had they here? All this you may understand better if you look at the map, and see where Tunisia is. You see that it lies close alongside of Algeria, of which the French have been in possession since 1830. As they strengthened themselves along the coast and in the interior, building towns and cities, how natural that they should look over the border at the neighboring territory, as Ahab looked at Naboth's vineyard! What an addition it would be if they could only get hold of it! That would carry the French possessions eastward, clear to the sea, and round out their African empire.

But, unfortunately, the country did not belong to France any more than it belonged to the United States. It belonged to Turkey, as the Sultan claimed every other piece of territory lying along the Mediterranean, except Morocco, which has a Sultan of its own. And his authority was acknowledged by Tunis, whose Beys ruled in the name of the Grand Caliph, who sat in state on the Bosphorus.

This made it awkward for France to seize a country that belonged to a power with which it was not only at peace, but in the most friendly relations. The thing must be done in some roundabout way, so as to secure the result, while professing to act only in the common interest of both countries. All that was wanted was a pretext, and that was easily found. In the mountains between Tunis and Algeria was a tribe that were said to be lawless and troublesome. Very likely they were. Living as they did on the frontier, the temptation was great to make incursions into Algeria, forays that were overlooked by the French until the moment when they could be turned to good account. But such border ruffians are not peculiar to Africa. The Highlanders who made descents upon the Lowlands for the purpose of cattle-lifting, were very much the same sort of freebooters as are the horse thieves who infest the ranches of Texas and Arizona. But we do not consider ourselves responsible for these marauders. No more was Tunis for these brigands. But no matter, it was sufficient for an excuse; and suddenly French troops were marched into these African highlands, and, when the moment of action was come, were moved on Tunis itself, where they presented their compliments to the Bey, and gave him just two hours to sign a treaty placing himself under the protection of France! Not to wound his dignity, this was under the phrase of "constituting the representative of France the medium of communication with other powers!" That was a delicate way of putting it. It saved the pride of the Bey, and softened the affront to Turkey. Not a word was said of annexing the country! Oh, no! but only that it should be governed through the representatives of another country. Some may speak of this disrespectfully, as "whipping the Black Gentleman round the stump;" that is, doing indirectly what they did not dare to do directly—keeping up professions and appearances, while dividing the spoil. Of course, those who profited by this piece of legerdemain, thought it a wonderful stroke of policy, while the other powers that gained nothing by the change lifted up their hands in holy horror at the base treachery!

Well, it must be confessed that it was a piece of sharp practice. As to any right in the case, France had just as much right to force this treaty upon the Bey as she had to land an army in Ireland, to stir up insurrection.

And yet England could say nothing, for the obvious reason that France would reply that she had done no more in Africa than England herself had done over and over again in India. Indeed, we have not been so very scrupulous in respecting the rights of the Indians to their lands. Perhaps we had better drop the subject.

In case of revolution we are apt to think more of the ruler than of his people, and to spend our sympathies on the one man who is turned out of his place rather than on his subjects, who may be set free from an odious tyranny. It did seem a little hard on the Bey of Tunis that he should be sent adrift on two hours' notice. But he was not quite turned out of house and home, but simply retired on a royal pension, with a palace to live in. I have just been out to see it, and after spending an hour in walking through the apartments, I could not but think that with his generous allowance from the French Government, with French servants to wait on him, and French cooks to supply his table, the poor Bey might still be able to support existence. Further yet, with French soldiers to keep guard around his palace, and French officers to form his military household, he could still keep up a miniature court; and if he could be no longer a grand bashaw, could still be a grand puppet.

And so I am not going to waste any tears on the Bey of Tunis, for the less there is of such government in the world the better. Macaulay has laid it down as an axiom, based on all his knowledge of history, that the best Moslem government is worse than the worst Christian government. When I was here six years ago, a French gentleman drove me out to the Bardo, a palace of the Bey two or three miles from the city, which was reserved for his official duties. Here he came once a week to sit in the Hall of Justice (or Injustice), to give judgment in cases between his own people, in which he was both judge and jury, and could render a decision which was absolute and final. He had the power of life and death over his subjects. If for any cause, or for no cause at all, but merely to extort money, or to gratify personal hatred, he saw fit to pronounce sentence of death, no man could ask the reason why. He need not take counsel of anybody; he need not even open his lips; he had only to wave his hand, and the miserable wretch was at once seized by the executioners. The sentence was carried out on the spot, in a court of the palace, where the condemned was thrown on the pavement, and strangled with the bowstring, or small cord, which was twisted round his neck till life was extinct. This judgment was executed under the eye of the Bey, who, it was said, sometimes left the bench, and came to the window to witness the dying agonies of the wretched victim. This was Oriental justice! I think my readers will agree, that, if there is to be any progress in the world, such a government as that must go.

But if the Bey of Tunis had to go, there was a question who should succeed him. France was not the only power that had cast longing eyes on Tunis. Italy considered herself the natural heir to the property, not because she was next of kin, but nearest in position, with the great island of Sicily lying midway between Europe and Africa, as a sort of bridge to connect the two portions of what might be one great empire. Thousands of Italians had come over to make their home on this side of the Mediterranean, so that Tunis had already a considerable Italian population, all of whom looked forward to the time when, in the natural course of events, the native government should break down, and the country fall to them without any act of violence or usurpation. The government at Rome was only observing the proprieties in waiting for the time to come, when the French stepped in, and, by a sudden *coup*, carried off the prize, leaving the Italians in the lurch. As a Frenchman in Tunis said to me, with evident exultation, "*Ils sont arrivés trop tard!*"

Too late, indeed! Too late to gain the coveted possession, but not too late for the consequences both to France and Italy, whose relations to each other it severed at once. Up to this time no powers on the continent had been more closely united. The two countries touched each other. The two peoples were of the same Latin race. Kindred in origin, in blood, in language, and in religion, they seemed formed by nature and by position to be allies and friends. They were also alike in their political sympathies, both being among the liberal powers of Europe, as against the absolutism of Germany, Austria, and Russia. Hence it seemed, that, whatever occurred in European politics to divide other nations, these two would stand by each other. France, too, felt that she had a claim upon Italy for the support she gave to Sardinia in the war with Austria in 1859, which gained Lombardy, to which, seven years later, France added the free gift of Venice. That Italy should not now acquiesce in the good fortune of her former benefactor seemed to the French base ingratitude.

But nations, like individuals, are more apt to remember injuries than favors. No explanations or apologies can soothe a bitter disappointment. Italy felt that she had been outwitted by France, which had taken from her the prize on which she had set her heart, and compelled her (as she was still ambitious of a hold in Africa) to seek it far away, on the shore of the Red Sea, in Massowah, one of the hottest and most unhealthy places in the world.

Nor did the irritation of Italy end here. It led her to cut loose from the power nearest to her, and to join her fortunes with Germany and Austria, as against France and Russia; so that, should we live to see the outbreak of that general war for which all Europe is looking and preparing, we may see Italy take the field against the old ally to which she owes her very existence.

But I am not a prophet of evil, and will not mutter forebodings of wars that may never come. What is of more interest to me, now that I am in Tunis, and find that the thing is done, and cannot be undone, is whether this change of rulers was a good thing. Was it good for Tunis? Was it good for France? Or was it good for neither? Was it a cheat all round? Or was it a good all round? I claim that it was; that it was a bargain which was for the profit of all concerned.

First of all, Was the country worth taking? Is it not for the greater part barren sea-coast, or still more barren desert? So high an authority as Sir Lambert Playfair thinks it very inferior to Algeria. There are fewer hills and more plains. "The mountain ranges nowhere attain so great an elevation; the country is less wooded; the rainfall is less; and a great part of the land is, if not absolutely sterile, capable only of yielding abundant harvests when stimulated to fertility by more than the usual amount of rain." And yet this very country was once highly cultivated, and sustained a dense population. He says: "It is extremely difficult to understand how the

Sahel [the region of wide, dreary plains] could have supported the immense population which it must have contained during the Roman period. It is covered in every direction by the ruins, not only of great cities, but of isolated posts and agricultural establishments. In many parts one cannot ride a mile in a day's journey without encountering the ruins of some solidly built edifice."

But what does France give to the country in exchange for what she gets? First of all, she gives law and order, the first condition of civilization. Wherever she lays her strong hand, savagery disappears. Of this Sir Lambert Playfair gives an illustration in one of the wildest and most savage parts of the country, the mountainous region occupied by the Khomair, the very tribe whose lawlessness led to the interference of the French. He tells us how, with one companion, he passed through that country in 1876, which he believed that no other European traveller had ever been permitted to do. He again traversed it in April, 1884, by excellent roads. Not an armed Khomiri was to be seen. The men were all engaged in ploughing the land for the next season's crops, while the women were clearing the weeds from among the growing corn; all seemed to have a friendly word or salutation for him, and he saw none of the black looks and scowls which he had noticed on his former journey.

All this is in the way of civilization. Where roads are opened through a country, and it is policed by troops which enforce law with military rigidness, there is every inducement to that peaceful industry which is the first condition of civilized society.

Next to the railroads and other roads which bind all parts of the country together, the greatest piece of engineering is in Tunis itself. A glance at the map will show that it does not lie on the sea, but at the head of a long, shallow bay, hardly more than a lagoon, which was quite insufficient for vessels to approach the city. They could come no nearer than the Goletta, six miles away, so that all articles of commerce had to be transported this distance to be shipped. Thus all trade had to be carried on at arm's length, at great expense of labor and money. To remedy this, and to make Tunis in reality, as well as in name, a port, the French undertook the building of a ship canal seven and a half miles long. It was a prodigious undertaking, but great dredging machines were anchored up and down the bay, and the work was pushed with all the energy and capital of France, with the assurance that it might be opened in 1894. It was completed a year in advance of the time, and in May, 1893, was formally opened, so that ships drawing twenty feet of water, instead of being obliged to unload at the Goletta, can steam up to the city, and discharge their cargoes on the wharves. This stupendous work alone, if there were nothing else, is a sufficient answer to the question whether the French occupation has been a benefit to Tunis.

So much in the way of commerce. But France is not a country that has an eye only to profit, but still more to power and glory. No one who reads the history of our own times can fail to see that, in assuming a protectorate over Tunis, she looked to the increase of her naval and military power. Napoleon used to speak of the Mediterranean as a French lake, an assumption that might have been thrown back as a bitter taunt after the battles of the Nile and Trafalgar, when his fleets were destroyed, and a ship hardly dared to fly the French flag from one end of the great sea to the other. Then England was mistress of the seas, and might have claimed the Mediterranean as her own. Especially with the fortresses of Gibraltar and Malta, to which has been added within a few years the occupation of Cyprus and Egypt, with control of the Suez Canal, she has a chain of strategic positions from one end of the Mediterranean to the other. How to neutralize this tremendous superiority, or to obtain at least some counterpoise to it, has long been the problem of France, which she seems at last to have solved. Neither Tunis nor Carthage offers any special advantage of position for attack or defence. But if the reader will turn to the map, he may find another point, not far away, which combines all the advantages that are wanting here. Less than forty miles distant, on the coast, is Bizerta, which seems to have been formed by nature, as much as Gibraltar itself, to be one of the greatest fortresses in the world. It is close to Cape Blanco, the most northern point of Africa, and has the supreme advantage of being directly in the line of all the commerce up and down the Mediterranean. Not a sail can pass in either direction without being in full view, unless it should keep away below the horizon to avoid being seen, or take the long sweep round the island of Sicily, and through the Straits of Messina.

But better still, Bizerta has advantages for defence not surpassed by Gibraltar itself; not in the outer port, but in a lake that lies behind it, separated only by a ridge of land, through which the French are now cutting a canal that will be completed next year, by which, says Sir Lambert Playfair, "the lake will be converted into a perfectly landlocked harbor, containing fifty square miles of anchorage for the largest vessels afloat." Here the fleets of France could ride in safety, and defy all the navies of the world, at the same time being ready to sally out and attack any hostile squadron that should come within their reach.

The bearing of all this has not escaped the notice of the military and naval authorities of other countries. Sir Charles Wilson, one of the first engineers in the English army, writes me, in answer to inquiries:

"Bizerta is admirably suited for a great military and naval post and arsenal; and the only question is, whether the French will so make it. It is believed that when the French occupied Tunis, there was a tacit, if not written, understanding that they would not fortify Bizerta and turn it into a first-class fortress and arsenal. I believe that thus far they have only thrown up a few field-works, but there is always the fear that the understanding will not be kept. The Italians are peculiarly sensitive to this question of fortifying Bizerta, and a year rarely passes without a debate on the subject in the Italian parliament, or some scare being raised in the European press. Bizerta is rarely visited by travellers. I was there many years ago, before the French occupation, and was much struck by its capabilities.

"The Mediterranean question, from a naval and military point of view, is a most interesting one, and has been much discussed of late years. Very great differences exist with regard to the present value of the great fortresses, and as to the effect of war upon the Mediterranean transit trade. The only clear point is, that the power or powers that command the sea will practically command the Mediterranean, and that this will be settled by a great naval battle. The fortresses will only play a minor part in the war; but there is no doubt that a great naval arsenal and fortress at Bizerta would be an unpleasant addition to the Mediterranean from a British or Italian point of view."

But enough of war, for just now my thoughts are turned on peace by some tender and sad memories. When I was here six years since, I was most kindly received by the Resident of Tunis, to whom I brought a letter, who made me at once at home, and, after we had discussed politics, would have me come the next day to meet his family. As we sat round the table the conversation took a wide range, and still more when we left the gentlemen to their cigars, and I accompanied his wife and sister into the garden, in the rear of the palace, where the paths led under the shade of some majestic trees, that looked as if a hundred years old. We talked of Africa and of America, which seemed to these French ladies very far away, while Africa was close to Europe. I invited them to visit our country and see the "Western barbarians," which amused them very much. All this comes to me now with a feeling of sadness, as I learn that that happy circle has been broken. The Resident, who was then in the full vigor of manhood, is in his grave, and his family have returned to France. It was a shock to me to receive the news on the very spot where they had given me such a kindly welcome, and I walked round the square and looked up at the old trees, under which we had walked and talked so gayly on that happy day, with grateful memories.

With these personal recollections there comes another of the honored dead. More than forty years ago there was an American Consul in Tunis, who died here April 1, 1852. Though his last days were spent far from his country, he sighed for the land of his birth, for which he had poured forth his love in lines that are perhaps as familiar as any in the language:

> "'Mid pleasures and palaces, where'er I may roam,
> Be it ever so humble, there's no place like home."

Here he was buried on a foreign shore; but after he had been in his grave over thirty years, his remains were disinterred and taken to America, and laid in the earth at Georgetown, near Washington, so that at last he sleeps in the land that he loved so well. But though he is no more, his words still live; and to-night, as I saunter through these crowded streets, I find relief from loneliness in thinking of those who are far away, and whispering to myself,

> "Home! sweet home! There's no place like home!"

CHAPTER XX

THE FALL OF CARTHAGE

WHEN Hiram, King of Tyre, took the contract to furnish the materials for building the Temple of Solomon, he showed not only his friendship for his royal neighbor, but the superior capacity of his own people. "For thou knowest," said Solomon, "that there is not among us any that can skill to hew timber like unto the Sidonians" (1 Kings v. 6). And so he is obliged to ask the aid of his brother king, whom he requests to command his skilled workmen to "hew him cedar trees out of Lebanon." Solomon was able to supply the manual labor, for which he "raised a levy of thirty thousand men, and sent them by courses, ten thousand a month;" but these must serve under the orders of the men of Tyre, who "could skill to hew timber," and who had also to engineer the transportation of the huge trunks that came out of the mighty cedars of Lebanon, as Hiram had said, "My servants shall bring them down from Lebanon to the sea, and I will convey them by floats unto the place that thou shalt appoint."

Equally dependent was Solomon for the ornaments of the temple on the men of Tyre, who were cunning artificers in all kinds of metal work, so that not only the sacred vessels, but the stately columns, and the molten sea, resting on the backs of twelve oxen, all of "bright brass," were wrought by the Sidonians. "So Hiram made an end of doing all the work that he made King Solomon for the house of the Lord."

Here is a bit of history that discloses the fact, that, after the Israelites had been over four hundred years in the Promised Land, and had reached the highest point of power and of glory under Solomon, they had, as their next-door neighbors, a people who excelled them, both on land and sea, in the arts of construction and in navigation. These were the Phœnicians, the men of Tyre and Sidon, who, at that early day, in the very dawn of history, were great builders and navigators, colonizers and civilizers, the founders of states and empires.

Such a people soon outgrew the place of their habitation, which was but a narrow strip of land on the Syrian coast, between the mountains and the sea; and sought a more central position, with more space around it, for a city that should be the capital of an empire. As they sailed up and down the Mediterranean, they came to know all its islands and its shores, and finally chose a position on a deep gulf, on the side of Africa, midway between the east and the west of the great sea; and here, eight hundred and eighty years before Christ, and more than a hundred before the founding of Rome, they laid the foundation of Carthage. Whether they followed the fortunes of an unhappy queen, Dido, who came hither to pour out her sorrows on this African coast, matters little. Romantic traditions that have been woven into the Æneid of Virgil it is better not to disturb. The important fact is, that it was one and the same powerful race that wrought in different parts of the Mediterranean; that as it was the men of Tyre who laid the foundations of the Temple of Solomon, so it was their descendants who, a hundred years after, laid the foundations of a city that was to become the greatest of the ancient world, and so continue until it was dethroned by Rome. The spot on which that historic city stood is but six miles from the modern city of Tunis, and a visit to it is the chief interest of this part of Northern Africa.

The access is easy, as it is but an hour's drive across the plain; or, easier still, the little Italian railway to the Goletta passes so near that it is but a short walk from the station to the foot of the hill, which you climb, and find yourself on the top of the ancient Byrsa, the Acropolis of Carthage, that was once crowned by the citadel and by the Temple of Esculapius, which stood in the very heart of the city, as St. Paul's stands in the heart of London.

The scene is enchanting. In the distance stretches the blue Mediterranean, with but a sail here and there breaking the line of the horizon. But could you transport yourself back twenty-five hundred years, the spectacle would be far more animated, as that horizon would be white with the sails of ships going to or coming from shores as far apart as Egypt and Spain.

In the nearer view, and almost under your feet, you look down on a broad and beautiful bay, with an open roadstead, the largest on the coast. A part of the bay that was more under the shelter of the land, and therefore more easy of protection, was divided into two harbors, an outer and an inner one. The latter was enclosed by a wall, and had an island in the centre, with quays and docks for over two hundred ships. Here were the arsenals, and here lay the Carthaginian fleet, composed of ships of all sizes, from the *triremes*, with but three banks of oars, to the *quinqueremes* and *hexiremes*, with five and six, requiring no less than three hundred galley slaves as rowers; besides a hundred and twenty fighting men. These were their line-of-battle ships, which were armed with iron beaks at the prow, and, being propelled with tremendous force, would break through almost any opposing line, and once at close quarters, the marines threw themselves on the enemy's decks and fought hand to hand. With such a navy it is not surprising that the Carthaginians kept so long the mastery of the sea.

But of more interest, even, than this warlike array in the harbor, were the ships of commerce which connected Carthage with all the ports of the Mediterranean, in Europe and Asia, as well as in Africa. Here lay the "ships of Tarshish," so called because they made voyages to Tarshish in Spain. Nor did the venturesome navigators stop at the Pillars of Hercules. Two thousand years before Columbus, the men of Carthage sailed out boldly into the Atlantic, extending their voyages to Great Britain and to the Baltic, and far down the western coast of Africa. It is even claimed that they pushed their way to the very end of the continent, and anticipated Vasco da Gama in passing round the Cape of Good Hope into the Indian Ocean. So Carthage became, and continued for centuries to be, the centre of a universal commerce, sitting, like Venice in the Middle Ages, as a queen upon the waters, and having poured into her lap the riches of all parts of the then known world.

Thus swelling in pomp and pride, the city grew till it had a circuit of twenty-three miles, which, if not so great as that of Babylon, yet enclosed more of wealth and imperial grandeur, because of the commerce which Babylon could not possess. Her merchants were princes whose villas and gardens covered yonder plain for miles.

The picture would be complete if we could know something of the interior life of the people. Mere wealth does not imply a high degree of culture. It may exist without general intelligence or elevated morals. It is here that we are left in ignorance of what we most wish to know, and what we do know in regard to some other ancient peoples. The great writers of Greece have preserved such pictures of their times, that we could take up our residence in Athens and feel at home, as we should be introduced into all the occupations of the ancient Athenians, even to their amusements, in which we could mingle with them in their public games. What would it be for us if we could be thus introduced to Carthage; if we could walk her streets; if we could look into the houses, or visit the shops and the markets, or go down to the wharves, and talk with the seamen just returned from Spain. But nothing of this have we, even in story. Carthage has left no literature. Books there must have been, for it was one of the accusations against the Romans, that they destroyed the public libraries, or suffered them to perish in the general conflagration. The Carthaginians, therefore, cannot speak for themselves; and it is their hard fate that even their history must be taken chiefly from their enemies. This fact puts us under the greater obligation to those who, out of such slender materials, have picked fragments of truth which they have woven into a connected narrative. Especial thanks are due to an English writer, Mr. Bosworth Smith, who, having given years to the subject, has produced a book entitled " Carthage and the Carthaginians." which may not only claim to be an authentic history, but which is written in a style that gives it a peculiar fascination.

But even though dead and buried, a city that stood so many centuries must have left some monuments of her greatness, which it is our first task to discover. But the enthusiastic traveller who comes here expecting to sit, like Marius, amid the ruins of Carthage, and meditate on the fall of empires, is surprised and disappointed to find that such ruins do not exist.

There remains, indeed, one monument of her imperial greatness, in the enormous cisterns that received the water for the city. I know it is generally supposed that these were not the work of the Carthaginians, but of the Romans after the conquest, when Carthage had become a Roman city. But even if it were so, it is quite probable that they were built, or rebuilt, on the ancient foundations; for nothing less great could have sufficed for the wants of a city that (as it had a population of seven hundred thousand after all the waste and destruction of two Punic wars) must have had, in the days of its glory, over a million inhabitants. Structures that are half underground are not expected to be imposing in architecture; but these are immense in size, a hundred feet long, spanned by arches of twenty feet, and twenty feet deep, which give us some idea of a city that could drink up such a river of water as was constantly poured into these reservoirs by an aqueduct that brought it from the mountains sixty miles away. The remains of this aqueduct, that still stretch across the plains like the broken arches of the Roman Campagna, furnish one of the most significant proofs of the greatness of this African city.

But this is all that Carthage has to show. Of the city itself nothing remains standing. This is a disappointment to the traveller. But he should remember that Carthage was not only taken, but destroyed so com-

pletely, that not only are there no temples like the Parthenon, and no palaces like that of the Cæsars, but not even a broken arch or column to mark the place where it stood. Indeed, all that is left of Carthage is its tomb, for as such we may consider the Byrsa, which answers to the Capitoline Hill in Rome, beneath which are buried the foundations of temples and palaces, all mingled in one undistinguishable ruin.

This is quite sufficient to show why there are no ruins of Carthage in a sufficient degree of preservation to be imposing, like those in the Forum at Rome. It has often been suggested that there should be excavations into this tumulus, as into that which covers the remains of ancient Troy. This has been attempted in a small way, but the work is expensive, and hardly justified by the result. But scattered fragments are found here and there, as weapons of war are picked up on a battle-field, that tell of the warriors who fought over it. There are household utensils and personal ornaments in silver and gold, that indicate the wealth and luxury of the ancient inhabitants. When I was here before, I had a letter to the archæologist sent by the French Government to make explorations, who had already begun a collection which he had arranged in a hall of the palace at Bardo. He took me to see it, and came with me also to Carthage itself, where he had gathered materials on the spot for a second collection. These, though not to be compared with those in the museums at Rome and Naples, are, so far as they go, full of interest and of suggestion of what may yet be discovered. Here one may see mosaic pavements, like those of Pompeii, that were trodden by the warlike Carthaginians, and fragments of columns and architraves, that give some idea of an architecture that resembled, if it did not equal, that of Rome; and the ornaments, some of them exquisite in design, wrought in gold and studded with precious gems, that hung on the necks of the Cleopatras of Carthage nearly three thousand years ago.

This desolation is more eloquent than any ruins could be. No one can stand upon the grave of an empire without asking, Whence came the overthrow of all this greatness? It is the old story of pride going before a fall. Had she been content to be simply prosperous, there might have been no end to her prosperity, for she led the commerce of the world, and the riches of all lands were poured into her lap. But it was not enough that she was rich above all other nations: she must be above them in political power; she would have no rivals; she must be first on land and sea. So completely was she mistress of the Western Mediterranean that she suffered no intruders. Any strange sail was pursued as a corsair, and when captured, master and crew were thrown into the sea. So long as she was strong enough to enforce her will, it was the indispensable condition of peace with Rome, that Roman ships should never pass Cape Bon. Nor were the grasping Carthaginians content with this: they would be lords of the isles as well as lords of the sea. Malta was a refuge for the ships of Carthage, as it now is for the ships of England. Then Corsica was taken, and Sardinia. But the greatest prize of all was the large island of Sicily, lying between Africa and Europe, of which Carthage took the western half, and would have taken the whole but that the eastern coast had been settled by the Greeks, who were as brave and daring as the Carthaginians, whom they defeated in one battle, with a loss of a hundred thousand men ; while their countrymen at home, in the same year and on the same day, destroyed the fleet of Xerxes at Salamis, a double victory for Greek civilization. This contest for Sicily led to a series of wars extending, though with intervals of peace, over two hundred years.

But all this was only preliminary to the life-and-death struggle with Rome, in which the two greatest powers in the world put forth their utmost strength to destroy each other. Who does not know the melancholy story? Is it not written in the chronicles of the Punic wars? The first of these (for there were three of them) lasted twenty-three years, and ended then only from mutual exhaustion, when Rome and Carthage agreed to be at peace, but which was really but an armistice, a breathing spell to make ready for a fresh contest; for at the end of twenty-two years the struggle was renewed, and continued for eighteen years, making in all forty-one years of battle and of blood on land and sea.

It is not the business of a traveller to tell the story of old wars: that belongs to the historian. But there is one figure that appears on the scene, that cannot be so lightly dismissed—a figure as great in that age as Napoleon in ours. Indeed, there are many points in which the career of Hannibal resembles that of Napoleon. Both had hardly reached manhood when they were placed at the head of great armies. Napoleon was but twenty-six when he took command of the army of Italy; Hannibal was but twenty-six when he took command of the Carthaginian army in Spain. Napoleon was but thirty when he led his soldiers across the Alps; Hannibal was but thirty when he led a far larger army a far longer march, in which he crossed the Pyrenees before he crossed the Alps, and on his way from one to the other crossed the Rhone; and Napoleon himself tells us that there is nothing in war more difficult than crossing a wide river in face of an enemy.

The great achievement of that war, and one of the greatest ever known in war, was the crossing of the Alps, in which Hannibal led the way for Napoleon to follow more than twenty centuries later, but in which the imitation was by no means equal to the original. Napoleon had not to go far to find the enemy or the field of battle. He had his own capital as his base, where he had a French army all ready at his command, which had only to march through French territory, and therefore in perfect security, to the foot of the Great St. Bernard. Even when he descended into Italy he was on familiar ground, where he had fought battles before. Hannibal had never seen the country he invaded, which he reached only by the most circuitous route through Spain and Gaul. Part of his army were from the other side of the Mediterranean: men of different races, speaking different languages; some of them were barbarians. The famous Numidian cavalry must have been recruited from the tribes of the desert, as they rode their horses, like our Comanches, without saddle or bridle, yet with such wild fury as swept away the knights of Rome. Such was the strange, miscellaneous host that Hannibal set in motion with all the incumbrances of war, with its horses, and even its elephants,* to scale the moun-

---

* This use of elephants in war is a reminder that the people who had such an attachment to their army came out of Asia, bringing with them the military habits of Eastern monarchs, who went to war not only with horses and chariots, but with elephants. It is a singular fact that while the elephant is a native of Africa, and that in some parts of the interior there are vast herds that rove in the forests, as the buf-

tain barrier that lay between them and the Roman territory.

History has given the details of that terrible march. It was a new experience for those accustomed to the burning sun of Africa to find themselves amid the snows, their half-naked bodies shivering in the winds that swept over the Alpine heights. Now they found themselves in a narrow defile, where hidden enemies could roll down

---

faloes once roamed on our Western plains, yet the elephant has never been domesticated for use in peace or in war. But cross over to India, and the elephant is a beast of burden almost as much as the horse or the camel, and is always an imposing figure on occasions of state. When the Prince of Wales was making his royal progress through India, every maharajah who was honored by his visit met him at the city gates with a train of elephants, the hugest of which was reserved for the prince, and when covered with cloth of gold seemed not an unworthy emblem of the colossal power that was personified in the heir to the throne. At the Camp of Exercise at Delhi, elephants drew the cannon upon the field, and then, forming in line, threw up their trunks in air, and trumpeted aloud their homage to the majesty of England.

That they would be used in modern warfare is doubtful, since it has been found, even in India, where an elephant is supposed to be trained to do anything and stand anything, that they are badly demoralized by explosives. At the battle of Plassey, Surajah Dowlah had a large force of elephants to drag the cannon on the field, but as soon as they were struck by shot from the guns of Clive, they turned to flight and rushed away, trampling down the ranks of the Indian army, and helping Clive to gain his victory. From this it would seem that they did not stand fire so well as ordinary cavalry. But in ancient times there was no thunder of cannon, so that the strength of the elephant might be made of service in a line of battle. However that may be, the fact that they were domesticated three thousand years ago ; and that in the stables of Carthage, with the four thousand horses kept for the Numidian cavalry, there were three hundred elephants : and that elephants formed part of the army of Hannibal, is proof sufficient that the men of Carthage, though they lived in Africa, were not Africans, but came out of Asia, bringing with them the military customs of the East, even to this peculiar feature of "the pomp and circumstance of war."

rocks upon their heads; and again they were stopped on the edge of a precipice till they could cut a path in the side of the cliff, by which they could creep around it in single file, and then widen it a few feet more till they could pass the horses and the elephants.

This was a test of endurance that would have demoralized an army that was at once half frozen and half starved, if it had not been inspired by the example of its leader. But where he led the way, his African soldiers could follow, till at last they reached the summit, and saw the streams running to the south, and in the distance caught the gleam of green valleys, to which the great commander pointed with one significant word, "There is Rome!"

But though the obstacles of nature were overcome, yet this bold invasion of the enemy's country seemed an act of madness. The army of Hannibal had been reduced to less than one-third of that with which he set out from Spain. Then it counted ninety thousand infantry, twelve thousand cavalry, and thirty-seven elephants. Now, of all that brilliant array, he could muster but twelve thousand infantry and six thousand cavalry, to which the Romans could oppose many times the number, besides the immense advantage of fighting in their own country. Yet Hannibal never hesitated a moment, any more than Napoleon hesitated, when he had crossed the Alps, to push on to fight the battle of Marengo. Both leaders knew their men and knew themselves; and in both cases the result justified their confidence.

For a time Hannibal moved from victory to victory, till in the battle of Cannæ he not only defeated, but annihilated, the Roman army. Fifty thousand men lay dead upon the ground. Then it seemed as if the hour of judgment had come upon haughty, imperial Rome; and if, in that moment of terror and dismay, he had marched upon the city, it appears to us, at this distance of time, that it must have fallen, which might have changed the history of the world. But that was not to be. After a brief paroxysm of despair, the old Roman courage and constancy returned in the resolve that the state should not die. As Carthage sent no reënforcements to Hannibal, he had to move slowly, and the delay in pushing his victory gave time to recover from defeat, and soon the tide began to turn. It is the highest proof of his consummate generalship, that, left unsupported, he maintained himself in Italy seventeen years. But by that time Rome had grown so strong that she was able to carry the war into Africa, and Hannibal had to return for the defence of his country, and fought his last battle against Scipio, when "the hero of a hundred victories suffered his one defeat."

Here ended the military career of the great Carthaginian, and here again we find a parallel with that of Napoleon. Hannibal fought his last battle, at Zama, when he was but forty-five years of age; Napoleon fought his last battle, at Waterloo, when he was but forty-six. But that which was the end of Napoleon only gave another opportunity to show the greatness of Hannibal, who could step down from the head of his army to the place of a simple citizen, without loss of dignity, and was at once elected to the highest office in the state, and showed that he was able to render services to his country in peace as well as in war. But the terror of his name was still felt at Rome, which, even when victorious, was not quite secure so long as her great enemy might again appear in the field, and made a demand for his surrender, so that to relieve his own people, he chose the alternative of voluntary exile, and left the country which he was never to see again. Sailing up the Mediterranean, he visited Tyre, the cradle of his race, from which he went into Asia Minor, pursued everywhere by his unrelenting enemy, till at last, when the King of Bithynia, overawed by the mighty power of Rome, was about to surrender him, he took poison, which he had long carried concealed in a ring, and so ended his marvellous history. Again comes the parallel with Napoleon. Both died afar from the land of their birth: Hannibal not in Africa, but in Asia; and Napoleon not in Europe, but far away, in the Indian Ocean, on the rock of St. Helena. Years after his body was brought back to Paris, "to repose," as he had wished, "on the banks of the Seine, among the French people whom he had loved so well." Carthage could not give to Hannibal even a grave. And he, in turn, could leave to his unhappy country only the memory of his patriotic devotion and the glory of an immortal name.

There is nothing sadder in history than the record of lost opportunities. If, after the close of the second Punic war, Rome had yielded anything to conciliate the pride of her adversary, there might have been lasting peace. But Rome never knew the virtue of magnanimity. The surrender was attended with every circumstance of humiliation. The last blow was the burning of the Carthaginian fleet, in which five hundred ships were towed out of the harbor and committed to the flames, in the sight of the whole population, that watched the destruction with a bitterness that could hardly have been greater if it had been the burning of the city itself.

Thus, at the very moment that Carthage was forced to

submission, she was stripped of the means, not only of resistance, but of maintaining her dignity, a position most galling to a proud and high-spirited people. Not even the death of "the dread Hannibal," as Livy calls him, which would have awakened a feeling of respect in the breast of a generous foe, could abate the old hatred of Rome, which now began to contemplate something more than conquest, even extermination! Old Cato, honest, but stern and unrelenting, paid a visit to Carthage, and finding that she had resources left that would make her still a dangerous rival, came back to Rome with this word upon his lips: "*Carthago est delenda!*" ("Carthage must be destroyed!") with which he closed every speech in the Roman Senate. It was easy to find a pretext for a new invasion. Carthage, reduced in territory, had been left to be attacked by its African neighbors, and when she resisted, was called to account for making war without permission of Rome, which demanded as guarantees for the future three hundred hostages from the noblest families of Carthage, and the surrender of all weapons of war; *after which* it was announced, as the decree of Rome, that the city must be levelled with the ground, but that the inhabitants might build another city anywhere along the coast, only that it must be ten miles from the sea! This drove them to the last extremity. They could but die, and they would die in defence of their altars and their fires. Returning within the walls of their city, from which every weapon of war had been taken, they organized one of the most heroic defences in history, which kept the Romans at bay for two years, and was ended at last only by a second Scipio, who was to win the title of Africanus, at the head of a great army. As we stand here on the Byrsa, and look across the bay, we can see the very point of land on which Scipio disembarked (not choosing to attack the city in front, but to make a sweep around it, so as to approach it from the rear), and can follow the line of march till we see the mighty host encamped beyond the walls, with the Roman eagles flying over them.

The issue was inevitable. Carthage had no longer a Hannibal to defend her. By regular approaches the besiegers closed in upon the doomed city. When they had breached the walls, and made an entrance, the people fought with the fury of despair, even while the city was on fire. As in the burning of Moscow, the flames, when extinguished in one part of the city, burst out in another, so that it was kept burning for seventeen days. And all the while the battle went on. The people fought from street to street, till at last, as the combatants grew fewer, there were but some fifty thousand driven into the citadel, who surrendered, to go forth from their proud capital as captives and slaves, while the merciless conqueror ploughed up the very ground where the city stood, and sowed it with salt, that it might not even bring forth the products of nature, in token that the enemy of Rome, after its struggle of a hundred years, had been blotted out of existence.

The fall of Carthage is the most awful tragedy in the history of the world. Other cities have been taken by storm. Garrisons have been put to the sword. Women and children have been massacred by a brutal soldiery. But never before did one blow destroy a race and a civilization. From this time the Carthaginians disappear from history. The second power in the world—a power that had flourished for seven hundred years—is swept from the face of the earth!

But overwhelming as the end was, if it had been a war of civilizations, in which one or the other, Carthage or Rome, must perish, there can be little doubt which it was better, for the interests of mankind, should survive. With all that was great in Carthage, with its commerce and its wealth, we cannot forget that the men of Tyre, who founded it, brought with them the worship of Baal-Moloch, with its ghastly offering of human sacrifices, and that the drums which drowned the shrieks of victims in the valley of Hinnom were heard also on these shores. Nor was it only their enemies, captives, or slaves that were thus sacrificed, but the fairest of their own sons and daughters, as the only offering with which Moloch could be appeased. Thus their very religion was an education in cruelty. The religion of Rome, with all its false gods, was not so cruel and bloody as this.

And there was in the Roman state an element of civilization, which its conquests were to spread over the ancient world. Its dominion was a dominion of law. It is the Roman law which is the foundation of the codes of all modern states, and if we may, without presumption, interpret the intent of the Great Ruler in the ordering of human affairs, it was that Roman civilization should prevail over the world; that the reign of law should prepare the way for the reign of peace; when, in place of one universal dominion, there should be a universal brotherhood.

The date of the fall of Carthage was one hundred and forty-six years before Christ. For thirty years the city lay on heaps, a scene of utter desolation, when the Romans themselves began to clear away the ruins. Here Julius Cæsar planted a colony, and his successor Augustus (whose long reign of peace gave opportunity for such restorations) began to rebuild the city, which, though it never equalled its former splendor, grew to be the most important city on this side of the Mediterranean; and, as Christianity spread along the coast, it became the seat of a bishop, who was a kind of African pope. Here lived Cyprian, one of the Christian Fathers, and here was held the famous Council of Carthage in the year 252. But this dawning prosperity was destroyed by the Vandals, who, in 439, nine years after they had taken Hippo, captured Carthage, and held it for nearly a hundred years, till their power was utterly broken in a great battle by Belisarius, in 534. These successive wars so weakened the country, that it became an easy prey to the Arab conquest, and the city was destroyed by the Saracens in 698, after which followed the long, dark night of a thousand years.

This is almost a blank space in history. Yet there are gleams of light in this African sky. Even in the Middle Ages, when the darkness was deepest, the Crusades that passed on their way up the Mediterranean flashed a sudden light along these shores, if it were only to tell that Christendom still lived. To this very site of ancient Carthage came the noblest of the Crusaders, Louis IX. of France, in 1270, at the head of sixty thousand men. But he came only to die. A pestilence broke out in the army, and he was one of the first victims. It is significant of the changes in human affairs, that here, where civilization was overwhelmed by barbarism, and the religion of Mahomet drove out the religion of Christ, a chapel should now stand in memory of the Most Christian King. In this tribute all can join, not to the Crusader, nor even to the king; but to one who was among French kings what Marcus Aurelius was among

Roman emperors: who gave to the throne a greater dignity than it gave to him; who, in his pride as a sovereign, never forgot his duty to rule in justice and in righteousness. No matter what his country or his creed, the spot is sacred where such a man gave up his soul to God.

But St. Louis is not the only Crusader that France has sent to these shores. On this very spot is buried one who died only within the past year, who was as true a knight as ever marched to the rescue of the Holy Sepulchre: a man of such noble presence and military bearing that he might have been taken for a marshal of France. This was Cardinal Lavigerie, who had hot blood in his veins, but whose indignation was always against wrong, and, most of all, wrong done to a feebler race; and who traversed Europe, stirring the hearts of princes and people by his fiery eloquence, if so he might rouse them to undertake a veritable crusade to put an end to the African slave trade.

But Cardinal Lavigerie was not merely a great orator, he was a great organizer. He founded a religious order, that of the White Fathers (so called from their white monks' robes), for the special duty of penetrating the Sahara and the Soudan. It was a service of peculiar danger. The first who were sent out were massacred by the wild tribes of Bedaween. But the greater the danger, the greater the courage! This was never wanting. Not only was the order composed of picked men, but they were inspired by the spirit of their leader. No one could look in the face of that African lion without being made stronger and braver than before. As I came out of the Chapel of St. Louis, I met one whom I recognized by his garb, and addressed with the freedom that one always feels towards an old soldier. "Ah, *mon frère*, are you, too, one of the conscripts for the holy war?" to which he answered as a soldier answers to the roll-call, who waits only for his marching orders. "And your heart does not fail you?" I was thinking of the bones of his brothers now whitening the sands of the desert. He smiled at the suggestion of fear, or that he might shrink from any danger. "And when would you go?" "To-morrow morning!" was the instant reply. This is magnificent; and if the Church, Catholic or Protestant, can command the services of many of such heroic mould, another generation will not pass before the mountains of Africa will be made beautiful by the feet of those who publish the tidings of peace.

It is but a few months since Cardinal Lavigerie was pushing on this organization, for which he had gone to Algiers (where is the "Mother House" of the several convents or training schools), when, on almost the last day of autumn, as the leaves were falling, he ceased to breathe.

But though he died in Algiers, it could not claim his dust, for it was not his home. Though he had once been Archbishop of Algiers, yet ten years since, when Tunis was taken under the protection of France, in the general reorganization the bishopric of Carthage was revived, and was fitly assigned to the most eminent man in the Church, who had devoted his life to Africa; so that Cardinal Lavigerie, as Bishop of Carthage, was the direct successor of St. Cyprian, who suffered martyrdom more than sixteen centuries ago. Here he spent the rest of his days. But it was not a retirement for repose. His restless mind was as busy as ever. He founded a college that has five hundred students—not Catholics only, but

Protestants and Greeks and Jews, and even Musulmans. He built a chapel, *Notre Dame de l'Afrique*, and, last and greatest of all, began the erection, on the highest point of Carthage, of a cathedral, to which his ashes have been brought as its most precious treasure, and which now remains at once his monument and his tomb. As I stood by the marble slab that covers him, I read that illustrious name with the same veneration that I read the name of David Livingstone in Westminster Abbey. Here, as there, the tomb of the crusader will be forever a place of pilgrimage, to which will come the dusky sons of Africa, to stand with uncovered heads around the dust of the benefactor of their race.

Three days after this I left Tunis for Marseilles. As we stood out to sea, the ship's company were all on deck, looking back at the receding shores, on which the most conspicuous object was the cathedral, whose white walls, as they reflected the setting sun, shone like the gates of the heavenly city. The last glimpse of poor, dark Africa was of something bright, a bow in the cloud, the sign of a happier to-morrow.

CHAPTER XXI

A SOUND OF WAR

The twilight fading over the sea comes on so gently, and touches the spirit so softly, that one is apt to fall, like Ben Adhem, into "a deep dream of peace," from which it is a rude awakening to hear in the distance the sound of war. But only a few months have passed, and that sound is distinctly heard, far off, indeed, at the other end of the Barbary coast, but so near to Europe that it is echoed on the other side of the Mediterranean, where all are listening to know what it means, and what it may portend.

The cause was of the slightest. For two hundred years the Spaniards have held a small town on the African coast as a penal settlement, as if it were an additional security at home to transport their criminals across the sea. It did no harm to Morocco, for this imported population was certainly a very quiet one, as it was kept close within prison walls. I once spent a day at Melilla, where the steamer was anchored within a stone's throw of the fortress-prison, and not a face showed itself at the barred windows. The inmates could not escape if they would, and would not if they could, for it would be only to meet a worse fate at the hands of the fierce tribesmen, who would either kill them, or sell them into slavery.

But the possession of even this little bit of territory was an offence to the mountaineers, who are fanatical Moslems, and traditional haters of the Spaniards, and who suddenly swooped down upon them to drive them into the sea. Taken by surprise, they made a brave resistance, and held the position till they could be reenforced, while ships of war threw shells into the camp of the besiegers. This would not be of much importance, were it not that this sudden outburst of fury is a torch thrown into a mass of inflammable materials, from which the fires may spread over mountain and plain, till they sweep the country. Already it is said that the whole of Morocco is greatly excited, while the Spaniards are equally fierce for war. This is a critical position, which may end in a general war between the two countries, that could not go on long without involving other European powers, all eager to share in the dividing of the great estate.

But is Morocco worth fighting for? It is the greatest prize in the world! One has but to look on the map to see the extent of the country. It is larger than Spain; larger than France; larger than the whole German empire. Nor is it a barren waste. Though bounded on the south by the Desert of Sahara, it is not a desert itself. On the contrary, it is the ancient Mauritania, which, in the time of the Cæsars, was the granary of Rome. That fertility it retains, in spite of all the waste and neglect of two thousand years. The surface of the country is as diversified as our own. It is crossed by the Atlas Mountains in three great ranges, between which are boundless valleys and plains, whose fertility is like that of Minnesota and Manitoba, with a soil of five, six, and even ten feet of black loam. Those who have travelled in the interior have told me of riding through fields where the long stalks were above their horses' heads. Even with the wretched cultivation of the Moors, who barely scratch the surface of the ground, it yields enormous harvests.

Equally rich is the country in minerals. It is a land of silver and gold. The hills bring forth brass, and the mountains bring forth iron. It has enormous deposits of copper. The luxury of salt need not be denied to the poorest; while in the interior the natives have long been familiar with what they call "the fat of the rock," which is nothing but petroleum, gushing out in springs, or bubbling up from wells so deep and inexhaustible as to be sufficient to light up the whole of the Dark Continent.

And what the country can produce, it can transport. The mountains are so many reservoirs of what they gather from the clouds, and murmur with the streams that trickle down their sides, and form rivers that flow through the valleys, by which the riches of the interior can be carried to the ports of commerce; while on the open sea, Morocco has a coast line of hundreds of miles both on the Atlantic and on the Mediterranean.

A country of such magnificent proportions ought to be the seat of an empire. Not only should it be the head and front of Africa, but it should be one of the most powerful kingdoms in the world. Why is it not so? Are its people enervated by a pestilential climate? On the contrary, although it is farther south than Europe, the heat is so tempered by breezes from the sea, that towns on the coast are resorted to for health, wherever it is safe for Europeans to reside. If there be a country in the world where men should not suffer from the extremes of heat or cold, it is Morocco. Nor should any be hungry or naked in a land which brings forth everything for the service of man.

And yet this country, so rich by nature, is one of the

poorest in the world. It is not that the curse of God has fallen upon it, but only the folly and the wickedness of man. One cause is enough: the government is an absolute despotism—all power, even to that of life and death, is held in one iron hand!

No man on earth is fit to be entrusted with such power, lest he become a tyrant in spite of himself. And yet those who have had some opportunity of studying the character of the Sultan of Morocco tell me that he is by no means cold, pitiless, and cruel. Mr. Perdicaris thinks him "the best ruler that ever sat upon the throne of Morocco." He describes him as a man of majestic figure, and of a noble countenance, not defaced by passion, by hatred, or revenge, but softened, as well as saddened, by the melancholy expression that is common in Orientals; with an eye that indicates anything but a cruel nature. This we can well believe in looking at a likeness that I have reason to believe is the only one in existence that gives any just impression of the man.*

---

* This was a singular piece of good fortune. In Tangier I made repeated inquiries for a photograph of the Sultan, but could find nothing, good or bad. Sidna Muley Hassan, though he had been on the throne twenty years, had never been in Tangier but once, three years since. But even if he had lived there he would have allowed no one to take a likeness of his royal countenance, for the Moslems interpret the command not to make graven images to forbid it. But when he took his departure, as he rode out of the Kasbah, in the midst of a great procession, somebody who had a kodak took a snap shot at the crowd. This the American Consul sent to me after my return home, but I could make nothing of it; for though the Sultan was the centre of the procession, his face was hardly bigger than the head of a pin. I had it enlarged to the size of an ordinary photograph. But that only made its defects more conspicuous. For the one black spot blossomed out into a halo of blackness, in which I could only see a protuberance that must be the nose, since it was where the nose ought to be, with faint

The kindly spirit of the Sultan shows itself in private intercourse. The Italian minister told me that when he was about to embark for Italy, and came to take leave, the Sultan asked why he went; and being told that "it was to see his mother," answered, in his soft voice: "If I had the honor to know your mother I should tell her how proud she ought to be to be the mother of such a son," and desired to be remembered to her. "And," said the minister, "when he sent an embassy to Rome, he directed them to seek out the home of my mother, and to present to her the respects of the Sultan of Morocco." This is not the manner of a barbarian.

But whatever may be the natural instincts of the man, the form of government, of which he is the head, is too

---

traces of eyes above and mouth below. This was discouraging; but I was told of an artist who could make something out of nothing—that is, could take the faintest outline, and, by delicate touches here and there, develop it into something of human shape. He took it, and after a week or two brought me the black spot with all its vagueness cleared away, and in its place the full, rounded face of a man. It was a face worthy of a king!

But whether it had any resemblance to the real, living Sultan was another question. To determine this I sent it back to Africa, to be inspected by those who had often looked the Sultan in the face; and received a letter from the American Consul, in which he says:

"The picture of the Sultan is excellent. I showed it to the Governor of Tangier [the Bashaw], to the Moorish Minister of Foreign Affairs, and to the Chief Administrator of Customs; all of whom at once exclaimed 'His Majesty, our master!' kissed the picture, and said, 'May the Lord and Mohammed always bring him out victorious!' In fact, every one to whom I have shown it has pronounced it 'excellent,' and 'just like him!' The artist who enlarged it deserves great credit."

As the result of this long chase, I think I may fairly claim to be in possession of the best portrait of the Sultan of Morocco in existence, indeed of the only one that can pretend to be an authentic likeness of the greatest monarch of Africa.

strong for him. Its iron mask hides all human features, and its coat of mail stifles all human sympathies.

There are methods of administration that are the legacy of ages of misgovernment, to reform which is beyond human power. In all Moslem countries, while there is a great deal of religion, there is no law, or none but the Koran; and whether it shall work for the good of the people, or for oppression and cruelty, depends upon those who administer it. Here would be the best place in the world for civil service reform. But that would be taking altogether too much pains with a very simple matter. In the empire of the Sultan the office does not seek the man, but the man the office. There is no roundabout way of making application or drumming up voters. If a man wants an office, he goes for it, and pays for it as he would pay for anything in the market. Why should he not pay? He has no salary. He takes the office for what he can get from it; what he can squeeze out of the people; and the hand of a Moorish governor is very heavy, and he can squeeze very hard.

So in the administration of justice there is no attempt to hold the balance even. If a man has a claim against his neighbor, he goes to the Cadi, and of course, in the Oriental fashion, he takes a present. This he does not offer openly to him who sits in the seat of judgment, for that would be an awkward and unprofessional way of doing it; but a servant follows, and deposits it in some corner of the room, just in sight, though the incorruptible judge never turns his eye in that direction. But the man gets his case, and it has cost him but a small sum, for justice (!) is cheap in this country. But as he departs in triumph, his neighbor appears, and, behold, he hath something in his hand, which leads the Cadi to see things in

a new light, whereupon he reverses his former decision!
But the game is not ended, for thereupon the first suitor
returns and "goes one better." This tips the beam the
other way, till the Cadi gets new ideas of the immense
importance of the case, and, in order to be absolutely
just, without fear or favor, summons the two parties
before him on a certain day, when he will hear and
adjudge their cause, which both understand to be a
timely notice that whichever brings the larger bribe
shall receive the award! This is Moorish justice!

Even more shocking than this are the usages in war.
The Sultan is constantly at war, not with foreign powers,
but with rebellious tribes, and takes the field himself,
not to gain victories by pitched battles, but to let loose
the spirit of murder by offering a reward for the head
of every rebel that is brought to him. No other hint is
needed that they are to make no prisoners! If a
wounded rebel is found lying on the ground, he is not
carried to a hospital nor left to suffer, but' his head is
cut off on the spot, and carried to headquarters to get
the reward. If heads are plenty, it is an occasion for
rejoicing in the camp, and the cavalry come riding in,
carrying aloft on the points of their spears the bloody
trophies of their victory.

Nor is this the only use that is made of such trophies.
These heads are too precious to be thrown away or
buried in a potter's field, and they are put in brine like
hams! As this " pickling " of heads is unworthy of the
proud Moor, it is put upon the Jews, as a low caste that
are only fit for such degradation. A lady, who visited a
city in the interior, told me that she once saw a train of
donkeys saddled with panniers that were filled with the
heads of rebels! When these were " cured " they were

CAVALRY RETURNING WITH THE HEADS OF REBELS

mounted on spikes, and placed over the gates of the capital. This is barbarism indeed, to the verge of savagery! But it is the custom of the country; and the rabble of Fez, if deprived of the ghastly spectacle, might show their displeasure as did the Roman populace, if they could not have their fill of blood in the Coliseum.

Surrounded by such barbarians, what could the Sultan do, if he were the most enlightened ruler in the world? Already the ultra-Moslem party look upon him as leaning too much towards the hated foreigner. He cannot introduce any modern improvements, such as railroads or telegraphs. He cannot open trade with foreign countries. The English embassy that came last year, to negotiate a commercial treaty, remained in Fez for months, and returned without accomplishing anything.

The Sultan cannot control his own people. Probably no man in Morocco is more indignant at the madness of the Riffs at Melilla in making war upon the Spaniards without his authority. No doubt he would be glad to have the leaders in his power, and to hang up their heads over his gates. But the moment he should march against them, he would rouse the anger and hatred of all Morocco against himself. Already there have been mutterings in the mosques of Fez for his want of sympathy with the most fanatical party, a feeling which might attempt his assassination. He is aware of his danger, and surrounds himself with a guard, not of Moors, but of blacks from the Soudan, stalwart fellows, who are taken into the palace, and, being treated as favorites, become devoted to his fortunes. With these trusty guards always at hand, and a hard-headed Scotchman to drill his household troops, the Sultan may feel secure that he shall die in his nest.

But after him the deluge! So say they all at Tangier. Everything is rotten in the state; but how to get rid of it? And if the Moor is driven out, who shall come after him? There is no want of claimants for the succession. France, if she were left with a free hand, would undertake the conquest alone, that she might have Morocco to "round out" her African empire. But here is Spain, in sight of the promised land, and quite ready to pass over and possess it; while England, from the heights of Gibraltar, looks grimly down, determined that neither shall be able to fortify the African coast, and dispute her control of the Mediterranean. These rivalries may render concert impossible, and prevent any action, as they have done in another notable case. For a generation the question has been, What shall Christian Europe do with the Turk? And now it is, What shall it do with the Moor? In neither case has it done anything. The jealousies of Christian Powers have kept one Sultan on the throne of Turkey, and may keep another on the throne of Morocco.

But sooner or later the crash must come. But the conquest will not be an easy one. The Moor will not surrender at the first summons. He has acted a great part in history, and now if it is to be a struggle for existence, he will not perish without giving one more proof of his courage and his power. Nor will he fight his battles alone. It will be a holy war, a cry that will be taken up along the whole of Northern Africa. With such portents the century is drawing to a close. The clouds hang low on the horizon. With forebodings of the greatest of all tragedies, a war of races and of religions, the world looks across the Mediterranean to see the curtain rise.

www.ingramcontent.com/pod-product-compliance
Lightning Source LLC
Chambersburg PA
CBHW022335230426
43664CB00040B/1019